Steps
to the
Anointing

DAG HEWARD-MILLS

Parchment House

Copyright © 2008 Dag Heward-Mills

First published by Lux Verbi.BM (Pty) Ltd. 2008

Published by Parchment House 2011
5th Printing 2014

Find out more about Dag Heward-Mills at:

Healing Jesus Campaign
Write to: evangelist@daghewardmills.org
Website: www.daghewardmills.org
Facebook: Dag Heward-Mills
Twitter: @EvangelistDag

ISBN: 978-9988-596-23-1

Dedication
To
William Aggrey-Mensah
Thank you for your splendid art work and creativity. You have made an immense contribution to my books and media ministries over the years.

Contents

Chapter 1

Seven Reasons Why You Must Be Anointed

1. You must be anointed because no one can fulfil his ministry by natural might or by human power but only by the Spirit.

    Then he answered and spake unto me, saying, This is the word of the LORD unto Zerubbabel, saying, Not by might, nor by power, but by my spirit, saith the LORD of hosts.

    Zechariah 4:6

True ministry will be successful only by the power of the Holy Spirit. A false ministry operates at the level of a schoolteacher, lecturer, or a motivational speaker. Decide to become an anointed person and to enter into true ministry.

Lift up your ministry by the power of the anointing. Without the anointing, you can do nothing.

2. You must be anointed because even Jesus Christ waited to be anointed before beginning His ministry.

    Now when all the people were baptized, it came to pass, that Jesus also being baptized, and praying, the heaven was opened.

    And the Holy Ghost descended in a bodily shape like a dove upon him, and a voice came from heaven, which said, Thou art my beloved Son; in thee I am well pleased.

    And Jesus himself began to be about thirty years of age, being (as was supposed) the son of Joseph...

    Luke 3:21-23

This event marked the beginning of the ministry of Christ. Up until the age of thirty, we do not hear of Him. From this time, when the Holy Spirit (the anointing) descended on Him, Jesus began to preach, to teach and to heal.

3. **You must be anointed because even the apostles were asked to wait for the Holy Spirit (the anointing) before beginning their ministry.**

    And, being assembled together with them, commanded them that they should not depart from Jerusalem, but wait for the promise of the Father, which, saith he, ye have heard of me.

    Acts 1:4

What kind of ministry do you think you will have without the Holy Spirit? Even the great apostles who walked with Christ needed to receive the anointing in order to make it in ministry.

4. **You must be anointed because great prophets like Elisha asked for the anointing when given the opportunity to ask for what they wanted.**

Elisha recognized that ministry was accomplished only through the anointing. When Elijah asked him what he wanted, he said he desired a double portion of the anointing.

And it came to pass, when they were gone over, that Elijah said unto Elisha, Ask what I shall do for thee, before I be taken away from thee. And Elisha said, I pray thee, let a double portion of thy spirit be upon me.

2 Kings 2:9

He could have asked for many other things. He could have asked for Elijah's good name, Elijah's money, Elijah's properties, Elijah's car or even Elijah's wife. But after years of walking with Elijah, Elisha knew where the secret of his ministry lay. He knew that it was all about the anointing, so he asked for a double portion of it. Why do you seek something else when great prophets seek the anointing?

5. You must be anointed because King Saul was not transformed into "another man" until he was anointed.

Saul was transformed from an ordinary person into a king when he was anointed. In the same way, you will become a man of authority (a king) in the kingdom of God when you are anointed.

You may use other methods to manipulate and control people but you will never become a man of authority without the anointing. The anointing of the Holy spirit will transform you into another man.

> **Then Samuel took a vial of oil, and poured it upon his head, and kissed him, and said, Is it not because the LORD hath anointed thee to be captain over his inheritance?**
>
> **1 Samuel 10:1**

> **And the Spirit of the LORD will come upon thee, and thou shalt prophesy with them, and SHALT BE TURNED INTO ANOTHER MAN.**
>
> **1 Samuel 10:6**

6. You must be anointed because King David, the anointed psalmist and writer of Scripture, ascribed all his blessings to the holy anointing.

David attributed almost every aspect of his life to the anointing. Highly spiritual people recognize the powerful effects of the anointing on different areas of their lives.

In the eighty-ninth psalm, we find King David singing one of the most beautiful psalms of all. In it, he describes the powerful effects of the anointing on his life. He spoke of help, strength, establishment, exaltation, and authority as things derived from the anointing.

If the anointed psalmist derived all these things from the anointing, how do you expect to come by the same without the anointing?

Can you blame King David when he cried to the Lord, "Don't take the Holy Spirit from me."

Cast me not away from thy presence; and take not thy holy spirit from me.

Psalm 51:11

The Holy Spirit (the anointing) was the most precious thing to him.

7. **The anointing is essential because Moses refused to continue the ministry without it.**

If even Moses would not take one step without the anointing, how come you have the confidence to carry on in ministry without it?

In the book of Exodus, we see how Moses refused to carry on his ministry if God removed His power and anointing.

When Moses referred to the presence, he was referring to the anointing and the power of God.

And he said unto him, If thy presence go not with me, carry us not up hence.

For wherein shall it be known here that I and thy people have found grace in thy sight? is it not in that thou goest with us? so shall we be separated, I and thy people, from all the people that are upon the face of the earth.

And the LORD said unto Moses, I will do this thing also that thou hast spoken: for thou hast found grace in my sight, and I know thee by name.

And he said, I beseech thee, shew me thy glory.

And he said, I will make all my goodness pass before thee, and I will proclaim the name of the LORD before thee; and will be gracious to whom I will be gracious, and will shew mercy on whom I will shew mercy.

Exodus 33:15-19

Chapter 2

Fifteen Powerful Effects of the Anointing on Your Ministry

Then thou spakest in vision to thy holy one, and saidst, I have laid help upon one that is mighty; I have exalted one chosen out of the people.

I have found David my servant; WITH MY HOLY OIL HAVE I ANOINTED HIM:

With whom my hand shall be established: mine arm also shall strengthen him.

Psalm 89:19-21

In one of the most beautiful psalms of the Old Testament, King David sings about the blessings he received because he was anointed.

In my experience, I find that very few people are able to relate their blessings to the actual source of those blessings. They do not know where and how they came to be where they are and to have what they have. That is often the foundation of ungratefulness and rebellion. I think it is an important quality to be able to think deeply and to recognize the source of all blessings.

It is wonderful to read how David ascribes all kinds of advantages to the anointing. He treasured the anointing so much and would often refer to himself as "the Lord's anointed".

May God open your eyes to see the value of His anointing on your life and ministry!

I believe that if more ministers could see what the anointing did, they would desire it and seek it above everything else. If the anointing had such an effect on David's life, you must expect the anointing to have the same effect on your life and ministry!

1. **The anointing will result in you receiving supernatural help for your life and ministry.**

David felt that his ministry as a king was helped because of the anointing. He said,

> **...I have given help to one who is mighty...**

> **Psalm 89:19b, NASB**

2. **The anointing will cause you to be raised up to heights in ministry.**

David saw his exaltation as a result of the anointing.

> **...I have exalted one chosen from the people.**

> **Psalm 89:19c, NASB**

3. **The anointing will establish you in the ministry.**

You can see a clear difference between a ministry that has been established by God and one that is not established. King David became established because of the anointing.

> **I have found David My servant; With My holy oil I have anointed him. With whom My hand will be established...**

> **Psalm 89:20-21, NASB**

4. **The anointing will introduce strength to your ministry.**

Many times ministers are weak in their preaching and ministry. The strength of delivery and the power to change people's lives is simply not there. The anointing will remove all sorts of weaknesses from your life and ministry. King David felt he was becoming stronger because of the anointing. David said,

> **...My arm also will strengthen him.**

> **Psalm 89:21, NASB**

5. The anointing will protect you from deception.

An evil that plagues ministers is deception. Deception develops into blindness and hypocrisy in ministry. Many experienced ministers have huge blind spots. They are able to see and remove a small insect but cannot see a huge animal like a camel when it comes by!

> **You blind guides, who strain out a gnat and swallow a camel!**
>
> **Matthew 23:24, NASB**

Jesus severely rebuked experienced ministers for their deception, blind spots and resulting hypocrisy.

> **Woe unto you, ye blind guides...**
>
> **Matthew 23:16**

> **Ye fools and blind...**
>
> **Matthew 23:17**

> **Ye fools and blind...**
>
> **Matthew 23:19**

> **Ye blind guides...**
>
> **Matthew 23:24**

> **Thou blind Pharisee...**
>
> **Matthew 23:26**

However, King David felt that he overcame deception because of the anointing: "The enemy will not deceive him" (Psalm 89:22). May you be delivered from deception because of the anointing!

6. The anointing will deliver you from afflictions of the devil.

David believed that sickness and other afflictions could not affect him because of the anointing. You will experience health because of the anointing.

...nor the son of wickedness afflict him.

Psalm 89:22

7. The anointing will cause enemies who fight against you to be destroyed.

The Lord's anointed did not think the enemies were being destroyed because he was a good strategist. He did not think his military victories were because he had a great army. He did not even think that his enemies were weak or unprepared. David felt that he had victory over his enemies because of the anointing.

But I shall crush his adversaries before him, And strike those who hate him.

Psalm 89:23

8. The anointing will cause you to experience the loving kindness of God.

King David realized that God was being kind to him. He could sense divine favours and continual mercies. He believed that he experienced the loving kindness of God just because he was anointed.

My faithfulness and My lovingkindness will be with him...

Psalm 89:24, NASB

9. The anointing will establish you as a man of authority.

...And in My name his horn will be exalted.

Psalm 89:24, NASB

The horn was a symbol of the king's authority and the phrase, "his horn will be exalted" speaks of the establishing of the authority of a person. Authority is something you could take for granted till you lose it.

When Solomon died, Rehoboam his son was unable to maintain control over the country. People simply would not obey him nor serve him!

David recognized that he had great authority, which was a result of the anointing. David believed that he was able to exercise authority in his kingdom because of the anointing. May your horn be exalted and may God establish your authority and your calling. May you find it easy to lead and to establish control.

10. The anointing will cause you to expand.

I shall also set his hand on the sea And his right hand on the rivers.

Psalm 89:25, NASB

The Lord's anointed, King David, saw his ability to expand beyond the rivers and the seas as being a result of the anointing. God gave me a ministry that extended beyond my country. To see the fruits of my ministry I have to fly over many rivers and oceans. All this is a result of the anointing. David believed that he was able to expand his ministry beyond the seas and the rivers because of the anointing.

I see your ministry growing beyond the river boundaries of your country.

11. The anointing will cause you to develop a powerful relationship with God.

He will cry to Me, "You are my Father, My God, and the rock of my salvation." I also shall make him My firstborn...

Psalm 89:26-27, NASB

You see, everything you have is a gift. Even your ability to seek God and to find Him is a gift. The greatest gift a person can have is a close relationship with God. David recognized this and treasured the ability to relate with God.

Once again he knew the source of this gift. Long before the era of grace, he believed he enjoyed a father-son relationship with Jehovah because of the anointing.

12. The anointing will give you something eternal.

Also I will make him my firstborn, higher than the kings of the earth.

Psalm 89:27

David recognized that he was receiving something more precious than what the kings of the earth had. Something eternal! Something truly valuable! The anointing will cause your life to have eternal value. Your ministry will bear fruit beyond this earth and into eternity because of the anointing.

13. The anointing will cause you to have a covenant relationship with God.

...And My covenant shall be confirmed to him...

Psalm 89:28, NASB

Many people do not realize that God does not relate to everyone by covenants.

Do you have agreements with everyone you know? Your marriage covenant and other business covenants are very special agreements with special people! God chooses special people to have covenants with.

David believed he had a covenant relationship with God because of the anointing. May you be one of the special people with whom God has covenants!

14. The anointing will definitely affect your children.

So I will establish his descendants forever...

Psalm 89:29, NASB

You can expect the anointing to influence your children and bring them to God. All experienced parents know that only the power of God can turn a child in the right direction.

Most children abandon the childhood ideals that their parents instil in them when they become teenagers. Soon you realize that only the power of God can turn the child in the right direction. Depend on the anointing and your children will be established and become a praise in the earth.

David believed that even his children would benefit from the fact that he was anointed. Indeed the anointing affects the children.

15. The anointing will give you a long-lasting ministry.

His seed shall endure forever, and his throne as the sun before me.

It shall be established for ever as the moon, and as a faithful witness in heaven...

Psalm 89:36-37

Many ministries fizzle out after a few years. Many things that we build have no lasting value. It takes the power of God to cause things to survive and endure. The anointing will give you that edge in ministry. Permanence and longevity will be released into all that you do because of the anointing!

Chapter 3

One Step to the Anointing

God Decides Who Becomes Anointed

Are there only seven steps to the anointing? I don't think so. The anointing is the Holy Spirit. The anointing is the power of the Holy Spirit. Can there be seven simple steps to the Holy Spirit? If there are seven simple steps to this anointing, why haven't more people received the anointing?

When you talk about the anointing, you are talking about God. Can there be seven steps to God? Can God be accessed by following seven simple steps? Certainly not! He says in His Word,

> **Verily thou art a God that hidest thyself, O God of Israel, the Saviour.**
>
> **Isaiah 45:15**

God hides Himself and is not easily found. That is why you must ask before it shall be given to you. You must seek before you find and knock before the door is opened unto you.

Sometimes you will need to go beyond asking and begin to seek. Sometimes you will need to go beyond asking and seeking, and start knocking.

Years ago, I heard someone sharing about seven steps to the anointing and I was really blessed by the truths in that message. After soaking it in for years I realized that there were many more sets of "seven steps" to the anointing of the Holy Spirit.

In this book, I will attempt to share about some of the sets of "seven steps" to the anointing. In this chapter however, I want to show you the one step to the anointing that overrides all other steps in this or any other book. It is the step that involves the sovereign will of God. No matter how hard you work or follow certain principles, God divinely chooses whom He will allow to come close to Him.

Four People Who Understood the Source of the Anointing

1. Jesus Christ taught that God's promotion, power, and blessings are ultimately heavenly decisions made by God.

The mother of the sons of Zebedee desired that her sons sit at the right hand and the left hand of the Lord. Jesus answered and said they would have to drink of the cup of sacrifice first.

> **Then came to him the mother of Zebedee's children with her sons, worshipping him, and desiring a certain thing of him.**
>
> **And he said unto her, What wilt thou? She saith unto him, Grant that these my two sons may sit, the one on thy right hand, and the other on the left, in thy kingdom.**
>
> **But Jesus answered and said, Ye know not what ye ask. Are ye able to drink of the cup that I shall drink of, and to be baptized with the baptism that I am baptized with? They say unto him, We are able.**
>
> **And he saith unto them, Ye shall drink indeed of my cup, and be baptized with the baptism that I am baptized with: but to sit on my right hand, and on my left, is not mine to give, but it shall be given to them for whom it is prepared of my Father.**
>
> **Matthew 20:20-23**

But even after paying the price and drinking from the cup of sacrifice, the decision as to who sits on the left or the right is taken by the Father.

This means that no matter how hard you work and how much you sacrifice, there are certain things that are decided divinely.

Certain positions are given divinely.

No matter how many steps you take towards the anointing, it is God who decides whether you will be anointed or not.

2. King David understood that God ultimately decides who receives the anointing.

Blessed is the man whom thou choosest, and causest to approach unto thee, that he may dwell in thy courts: we shall be satisfied with the goodness of thy house, even of thy holy temple.

Psalm 65:4

God chooses people to come close to Him. God makes people approach His courts. David said, "...thou causest [them] to approach unto thee..."

3. It was revealed to Moses that the presence of God was given by God's own choice.

God's presence would be with you, Moses was told. Don't forget that Moses was a murderer wanted in Egypt for his crimes.

God had divinely decided to show him mercy. God chooses whom He will honour with His anointing and presence. Your sacrifice and hard work will not always earn you a place.

And he said unto him, If thy presence go not with me, carry us not up hence.

For wherein shall it be known here that I and thy people have found grace in thy sight? is it not in that thou goest with us? so shall we be separated, I and thy people, from all the people that are upon the face of the earth.

And the LORD said unto Moses, I will do this thing also that thou hast spoken: for thou hast found grace in my sight, and I know thee by name.

And he said, I beseech thee, shew me thy glory.

And he said, I will make all my goodness pass before thee, and I will proclaim the name of the LORD before

thee; and will be gracious to whom I will be gracious, and will shew mercy on whom I will shew mercy.

Exodus 33:15-19

4. Paul had this revelation too. He knew that God decides who will carry the anointing.

On the contrary, who are you, O man, who answers back to God? The thing molded will not say to the molder, "Why did you make me like this," will it?

Or does not the potter have a right over the clay, to make from the same lump one vessel for honorable use, and another for common use?

Romans 9:20-21, NASB

Chapter 4

Seven Steps to the Anointing in Jordan

Then cometh Jesus from Galilee to Jordan unto John, to be baptized of him. But John forbad him, saying, I have need to be baptized of thee, and comest thou to me? And Jesus answering said unto him, Suffer it to be so now: for thus it becometh us to fulfil all righteousness. Then he suffered him.

And Jesus, when he was baptized, went up straightway out of the water: and, lo, the heavens were opened unto him, and he saw the Spirit of God descending like a dove, and lighting upon him: And lo a voice from heaven, saying, This is my beloved Son, in whom I am well pleased.

Matthew 3:13-17

In the seven steps to the anointing in the Jordan, we see how our Lord Jesus received the Holy Spirit and became anointed for ministry. Within these few verses lie powerful revelations that will lead you to the anointing you desire. They are steps that our Saviour Himself took. They are the steps that lead to the highest kind of anointing.

The anointing Jesus carried was the anointing without measure.

Step 1: Go to Your Man of God

Then cometh Jesus from Galilee to Jordan unto John...

Matthew 3:13

God has an anointing for you and He will give it to you through His servant. Unfortunately, many people join the wrong church or ministry. In so doing they end up not receiving the anointing. Sometimes the person carrying the anointing you need is younger than you are or from the "wrong" country. Maybe he is black when he should have been white. Maybe his accent is different from yours and you despise him.

John the Baptist lived and ministered far away in the wilderness. He wore home-made panties as he ministered in public. He ate locusts and wild honey for lunch everyday. Yet this was the person that our Lord was attracted to. You must be attracted to the anointing. You must see beyond the physical. You must see beyond the unattractive human frailties and buy into the anointing.

Step 2: Submit to Your Man of God

Now when all the people were baptized, it came to pass, that Jesus also being baptized...

Luke 3:21

Jesus did not only attend John the Baptist's ministry; He submitted Himself to it. When everyone was being baptized, He joined them and received his blessing. He did not become a spectator and a commentator. He did not become a critic of John the Baptist's ministry. He was actually baptized by John the Baptist.

In other words, he actually followed the teachings and directives of John the Baptist. John was a man of violent preaching and water baptism. Jesus Christ joined fully and flowed with everything. When it was time for baptism, He went forward and participated. There are many people who do not follow the teachings and instructions of their spiritual fathers. They hang around and are associated with the ministry but do not actually submit themselves to what is being taught. You need to submit yourself to what is being taught.

Step 3: Humble Yourself in the Kingdom

When Jesus came to John, He humbled Himself and joined the ranks.

Now when all the people were baptized, it came to pass, that Jesus also being baptized...

Luke 3:21

Jesus joined the people and received His baptism as a commoner.

It is important to be humble in the church or ministry God has brought you to. Older, rich people rarely receive the anointing. It is difficult for people who are elevated in society to receive the anointing.

The master key to receiving anything in the kingdom is humility. Jesus said, unless you are humble like a little child you cannot enter the kingdom. Entrance into the anointing is granted through the key of childlike humility.

If Jesus had not humbled Himself and been baptized, He would not have received the anointing.

Step 4: Do Not Be Led by Men

But JOHN FORBAD HIM, saying, I have need to be baptized of thee, and comest thou to me?

Matthew 3:14

The fourth step of the anointing involves avoiding the mistake of being led by men. Do not let any human being keep you from doing anything you must do to become anointed. John the Baptist tried to prevent Jesus from being baptized.

You may be surprised to know that men of God sometimes give advice that directs you away from the anointing. The anointing is the most precious gift you can receive from God.

It therefore comes with the most stringent tests. Who would suspect that the words or advice of a trusted man of God could actually direct you away from the anointing. That is a difficult high-level test for anyone. We all know that the devil would love to prevent you from becoming anointed.

But this is what happened when Elijah tried to stop Elisha from following him. From Gilgal to Jericho to Bethel and even at Jordan, Elijah tried to get rid of Elisha.

This very difficult test shows whether the man desirous of the anointing is tuned to hear God's voice even in the most doubtful, vague and unclear circumstances. When you become anointed, you will have great authority and you must be in tune with God.

Step 5: Complete All Necessary Formalities and Fulfil All Righteousness.

There are legal requirements for you to be granted access to the anointing. Just as there are formalities that have to be completed for you to enter a school, a bus, an airplane or even a country, there are things you must fulfil in order to legally qualify for the anointing. It would have been a great mistake for our Lord to miss the baptism. His submission to John the Baptist's ministry was essential to legally establish His own authority. Years later, when Jesus' authority was questioned, He only made reference to John the Baptist and asked if they recognized John the Baptist's authority.

When John Wesley was challenged about the authority by which he preached, he declared that he preached on the authority given to him by his ordination under the Church of England. Every great minister must legally establish the basis for his spiritual authority as having submitted himself to the ministry of another man of God.

Unfortunately, many ministers deprive themselves of legal spiritual authority by not being properly ordained and ushered into ministry.

Step 6: Understand the Timings of God

And Jesus answering said unto him, Suffer it to be so NOW...

Matthew 3:15

The kingdom of God operates with times and seasons. Jesus knew that it was time to be submitted to someone else. There is a season for everything. To become anointed, you must discern when it is time for you to do certain things.

Sometimes we are afraid to relate to certain people or do certain things because we feel we will have to do it forever. Do I have to honour this man of God forever? Do I have to submit forever? Do I have to give an offering to this fellow every year?

What people do not understand is that there is a time and a season for everything. Jesus would live His life and conduct His ministry independent of John the Baptist. He would even preach and teach on a completely different theme.

However, at that time of His life and ministry, He needed to attend the meetings of John the Baptist and submit to the practices of John.

What are you supposed to do at this time? Do not abort your ministry by misbehaving during a crucial and humbling season of your life.

Step 7: Prayer and Spirituality

Now when all the people were baptized, it came to pass, that Jesus also being baptized, and PRAYING, the heaven was opened,

Luke 3:21

Pray for the anointing! Pray for the Holy Spirit! Prayer is an important step to receiving the anointing. If you pray and ask God for the Holy Spirit He will give it to you. Whilst the rest of the congregation were probably holding their noses to keep the water out, Jesus was praying. He prayed and the heavens opened and the Holy Ghost descended. Perhaps the most important prayer you will ever pray is the prayer for the anointing!

Jesus taught us to specifically pray for the Holy Spirit. This is a prayer for the anointing. The Holy Spirit is the one thing all ministers should pray for.

If ye then, being evil, know how to give good gifts unto your children: how much more shall your heavenly Father give the Holy Spirit to them that ask him?

Luke 11:13

The Holy Spirit will help us. The Holy Spirit will fall on us and our desert ministries will turn into green fields.

Ask ye of the LORD rain in the time of the latter rain; so the LORD shall make bright clouds, and give them showers of rain, to every one grass in the field.

Zechariah 10:1

The Coming of the Anointing

...and, lo, the heavens were opened unto him, and he saw the Spirit of God descending like a dove, and lighting upon him:

Matthew 3:16

Finally, the heavens opened and the Holy Spirit descended on the Lord. Then began the powerful ministry of our Saviour Jesus Christ. The power that would make mighty miracles happen had arrived. The power that would raise the dead three times was now present. The Holy Spirit had descended in a bodily form on Jesus Christ. He was no longer someone who had just taken up the form of a man; He was someone anointed with the Holy Ghost and power who went about doing good and healing all that were oppressed of the devil.

May you be anointed by the Holy Spirit! May you have the experience of becoming an anointed person! May you walk with God and follow Him until the day when the precious substance of the anointing is yours.

Chapter 5

Seven Steps to the Anointing in the Wilderness

And Jesus being full of the Holy Ghost returned from Jordan, and was led by the Spirit into the wilderness, Being forty days tempted of the devil. And in those days he did eat nothing: and when they were ended, he afterward hungered.

And the devil said unto him, If thou be the Son of God, command this stone that it be made bread.

And Jesus answered him, saying, It is written, That man shall not live by bread alone, but by every word of God.

And the devil, taking him up into an high mountain, shewed unto him all the kingdoms of the world in a moment of time. And the devil said unto him, All this power will I give thee, and the glory of them: for that is delivered unto me; and to whomsoever I will I give it. If thou therefore wilt worship me, all shall be thine.

And Jesus answered and said unto him, Get thee behind me, Satan: for it is written, Thou shalt worship the Lord thy God, and him only shalt thou serve.

And he brought him to Jerusalem, and set him on a pinnacle of the temple, and said unto him, If thou be the Son of God, cast thyself down from hence:

For it is written, He shall give his angels charge over thee, to keep thee:

And in their hands they shall bear thee up, lest at any time thou dash thy foot against a stone.

And Jesus answering said unto him, It is said, Thou shalt not tempt the Lord thy God.

And when the devil had ended all the temptation, he departed from him for a season.

And Jesus returned in the power of the Spirit into Galilee: and there went out a fame of him through all the region round about.

And he taught in their synagogues, being glorified of all.

Luke 4:1-15

Step 1: Being Led by the Spirit

Then was Jesus led up of the Spirit...

Matthew 4:1

To arrive at the place of the anointing, you will need to be led by the Holy Spirit. Most people think of the Holy Spirit as someone who leads us to different physical locations. You may think that the Holy Spirit will lead you to go to certain countries or cities.   But the Holy Spirit is leading you to a spiritual destination. Your destiny is to become an anointed person. Your destination is a pool of oil and ointment from the Holy Spirit!

Years ago, I heard Kenneth Hagin say that the secret that distinguishes ministers, one from another, is the ability to be led by the Spirit. From then on, I became very interested in being led by the Spirit. I believe it is one of the most important skills a person can acquire - the ability to be led by the Holy Spirit! I fell in love with Kenneth Hagin's book, "How to Be Led by the Spirit of God". I also believe that being led by the Spirit is the distinguishing feature of anointed men.

Indeed, Moses taught that the ability to hear the voice of God would cause Israel to be set apart and distinguished from other colleague nations.

> **And it shall come to pass, if thou shalt hearken diligently unto the voice of the LORD thy God, to observe and to do all his commandments which I command thee this day, that the LORD thy God will set thee on high above all nations of the earth:**

Deuteronomy 28:1

Do you want to be set apart and to become unique, prominent, outstanding, and even exceptional in ministry? Then learn how to follow the voice of the Holy Spirit. He is ready to lead you to the place of the anointing, just as He did with Jesus.

Step 2: Being Someone Who Can Be Led by the Holy Spirit to a Wilderness

Then was Jesus led up of the Spirit into the wilderness...

Matthew 4:1

The Holy Spirit led Jesus to a wild and barren desert - a place of hardship away from all comforts and delights. Yet Jesus followed the Holy Spirit to this difficult place. Most people will follow the Holy Spirit only if He is leading them somewhere nice.

You must become someone who has the ability to follow the Holy Spirit even when He is leading you against your natural inclinations. This is a higher level of being led by the Spirit. To be anointed, is to be endowed with supernatural, heavenly powers. These powers are not for games or for casual play. The anointing cannot be used for your personal interests. An anointed person must follow the Spirit and obey His instructions all the time.

If you have not learnt how to follow the Holy Spirit you will probably be a dangerous holder of the anointing. You would be like an irresponsible terrorist with nuclear weapons at your disposal. This is why you must first become someone who can be led anywhere, anytime, any day and even to your own death.

Step 3: Passing the Tests and Temptations of Ministry

Then was Jesus led up of the Spirit into the wilderness to be tempted...

Matthew 4:1

It is important to understand that God tests us so that He can promote us. The children of Israel were led through the wilderness by the pillar of fire.

Their first port of call was a pool of bitter water.

> **Then Moses led Israel from the Red Sea, and they went out into the wilderness of Shur; and they went three days in the wilderness and found no water.**
>
> **When they came to Marah, they could not drink the waters of Marah, for they were bitter; therefore it was named Marah.**
>
> **Exodus 15:22-23**

I believe that God will lead you to bitter experiences as part of His overall plan for your life. It will bring out the best or the worst in you. It will separate believers from non-believers. By the time you finish with the wilderness your faith will either be rock solid or you will be out of the ministry.

I remember one day when the Lord whispered into my spirit, "All that happened was a test." This was after I had struggled through various experiences for some years. I was indeed taken aback. It had not occurred to me that what I was going through was any kind of test.

Many of your experiences are simply tests on the way to the anointing. Allow God to take you through the wilderness and bitterness of ministry. Surely, it is but a step towards the anointing you desire.

Step 4: Passing the Tests of the Flesh

> **And when the tempter came to him, he said, If thou be the Son of God, command that these stones be made bread.**
>
> **But he answered and said, It is written, Man shall not live by bread alone, but by every word that proceedeth out of the mouth of God.**
>
> **Matthew 4:3-4**

Before you are anointed, you must pass the tests of the flesh. Jesus was tested with a temptation that involved his fleshly and natural desires. When you become anointed, the virgins will love you and men will give themselves for you.

Because of the savour of thy good ointments thy name is as ointment poured forth, therefore do the virgins love thee.

Song 1:3

The anointing will give you easy access to adoring multitudes. If you have not gained control over your flesh, you will sleep with many women or men before your life and ministry is over.

The anointing will eventually give you power and authority over much money. This relationship between finances and the anointing is a prophecy of Isaiah.

But ye shall be named the Priests of the LORD: men shall call you the Ministers of our God: ye shall eat the riches of the Gentiles, and in their glory shall ye boast yourselves.

Isaiah 61:6

In the day that you walk in the anointing and have access to the riches of the Gentiles, how will you behave? Will you steal all the money that belongs to God's church or will you control yourself? Will you exercise self-control over your desires and fancies in the day that you are anointed? This is why God tests your flesh on the road to the anointing. If Jesus was tested in that way, so will you be tested!

When you are an anointed person you cannot just do anything you want. It's that simple. You can't behave anyhow and do anything. You are under great restriction because of the anointing.

Step 5: Passing the Tests to Misuse Authority

Then the devil taketh him up into the holy city, and setteth him on a pinnacle of the temple,

And saith unto him, If thou be the Son of God, cast thyself down: for it is written, He shall give his angels charge concerning thee: and in their hands they shall bear thee up, lest at any time thou dash thy foot against a stone.

Jesus said unto him, It is written again, Thou shalt not tempt the Lord thy God.

Matthew 4:5-7

On the way to the highest anointing, you will be tested just as Jesus was. Jesus was offered the chance to misuse His power. He was tempted to use the power, finance, and influence of His ministry for something God had not called Him to.

He was tempted to use the influence of His ministry to accomplish some personal feat different from His assignment.

Sometimes, ministers use the influence of their ministry to build things which are not inspired by God. The anointing on Jesus was not for mountain climbing or cliff-hanging! Jesus was not about to use the gift of God to become the world record holder for high jump. Jesus was tempted to redirect spiritual energy into secular and social ventures. So it is when ministers direct the vast resources and influence of the ministry away from the Gospel.

Before you receive the mighty power of the Spirit, God will test you to see how much you will deviate from His calling when He gives you ultimate power and influence.

Step 6: Being Tempted to Take Short Cuts in Ministry

Again, the devil taketh him up into an exceeding high mountain, and sheweth him all the kingdoms of the world, and the glory of them;
And saith unto him, All these things will I give thee, if thou wilt fall down and worship me.

Then saith Jesus unto him, Get thee hence, Satan: for it is written, Thou shalt worship the Lord thy God, and him only shalt thou serve.

Matthew 4:8-10

On the road to the anointing, Jesus was also tempted to take short cuts. He was tempted to bow to the devil and take back the world He had come to save.

This was the shortest route to the salvation of the entire world. Through this short cut, He would not have to preach and travel to so many villages.

He would not have to suffer persecution at the hands of hateful men. What a quick way to achieve your dreams. This is a common test on the road to the anointing.

There is a way that seems right to a man but the end of that way is death. Sometimes it is not just about getting things done. It is about how the thing was done.

It is good to start a church, but how you start the church can affect the future. It is shorter and faster for you to break someone's church and begin your church with half of his congregation. But that short cut will not lead you to the anointing. There are many other short cuts that avoid humiliation, rejection, and accusations. Dear friend, through much tribulation we must all enter into the kingdom.

Step 7: Going to the Place Where Your Anointing Can Flourish

And Jesus returned in the power of the Spirit into Galilee...

Luke 4:14

The last step to the anointing is the wisdom to go to the place where the gift and anointing on your life can flourish. As you will notice, Jesus went to Galilee and not to Jerusalem.

Jesus basically ministered in the region of Galilee, which is a few hours drive from Jerusalem. Why did He not go to Jerusalem? He did not go to Jerusalem because the anointing would not work in that town. When He ministered in Nazareth, He was not received and was able to do very few miracles (Mark 6:2).

Years ago, I thought, "If you are anointed, you are anointed."

"If it is God, then He can work everywhere and with anyone," I thought to myself.

However, I have come to discover that God does not work everywhere with everyone no matter how strong the anointing is.

One of the most surprising Scriptures in the Bible is where Jesus lamented over certain towns. Those towns were described as places where He did most of His great works.

> **Then began he to upbraid the cities WHEREIN MOST OF HIS MIGHTY WORKS WERE DONE, because they repented not:**
> **Woe unto thee, Chorazin! woe unto thee, Bethsaida! for if the mighty works, which were done in you, had been done in Tyre and Sidon, they would have repented long ago in sackcloth and ashes.**
>
> **Matthew 11:20-21**

It is apparent that He did not do great works everywhere. Surprisingly, the Scripture tells us that he could not perform miracles in His own country where He had been brought up.

The Bible does not say He did not; it says He could not perform miracles there.

> **And he COULD THERE DO NO MIGHTY WORK, save that he laid his hands upon a few sick folk, and healed them.**
> **And he marvelled because of their unbelief. And he went round about the villages, teaching.**
>
> **Mark 6:5-6**

It is important for you to go to your Galilee. Do not go to Jerusalem or Nazareth. There is a Galilee waiting for you. It is in Galilee that you will find the greatest fulfilment. You will discover cities like Bethsaida and Chorazin where you will do great works for the Lord.

Do not try to be greater than Jesus. If Jesus did great works everywhere, then you can expect that too.

But He didn't and He couldn't! If Jesus did great works in certain places then expect to do great works in certain places. Just plug yourself into your Galilee and begin to prosper in the anointing.

Chapter 6

Steps to the Anointing in the House of Cornelius

There was a certain man in Caesarea called Cornelius, a centurion of the band called the Italian band, A devout man, and one that feared God with all his house, which gave much alms to the people, and prayed to God alway.

He saw in a vision evidently about the ninth hour of the day an angel of God coming in to him, and saying unto him, Cornelius.

And when he looked on him, he was afraid, and said, What is it, Lord? And he said unto him, Thy prayers and thine alms are come up for a memorial before God.

And now send men to Joppa, and call for one Simon, whose surname is Peter:

Acts 10:1-5

While Peter yet spake these words, the Holy Ghost fell on all them which heard the word.

And they of the circumcision which believed were astonished, as many as came with Peter, because that on the Gentiles also was poured out the gift of the Holy Ghost.

For they heard them speak with tongues, and magnify God. Then answered Peter,

Acts 10:44-46

Step 1: Giving Offerings to God

A devout man, and one that feared God with all his house, which gave much alms to the people, and prayed to God alway.

Acts 10:2

31

The story of Cornelius is the story of a man who miraculously received the infilling of the Holy Spirit. He was selected from his town, Caesarea, and anointed with the Holy Spirit. The passage in the book of Acts gives us a glimpse into the life of this special person who received the anointing. The first step in the progression of Cornelius' anointing was the fact that he gave to the Lord.

One who is gracious to a poor man lends to the LORD, And He will repay him for his good deed.

Proverbs 19:17

Being gracious to the poor was Cornelius' chance to give something to God.

...Thy prayers and thine alms are come up for a memorial before God.

Acts 10:4

These prayers and acts of giving to the poor caught the attention of the Lord. It is not my theory that giving offerings catches the attention of God.

The angel informed Cornelius that it was his alms (giving) and prayer that arrested the attention of God. Dear friend, the anointing that you seek and the help that you desire can be acquired when you learn this great act of worship.

Step 2: Give Offerings to the Poor

A devout man, and one that feared God with all his house, which gave much alms to the people, and prayed to God alway.

Acts 10:2

Giving to the poor is a special form of giving that is precious to the Lord. You will discover that most anointed people have a strong ministry to the poor.

Ministering to the poor does not remove poverty from the earth. Giving money to the poor does not usually solve the problems of poor people. That is not the issue here. God loves the poor and anoints people who love them.

Five Supernatural Benefits of Ministering to the Poor

David, the anointed psalmist knew that people who remember the poor would attract the power of God. David prophesied that those who helped the poor would be: (1) delivered and (2) kept alive. He declared that they would be (3) preserved, (4) blessed and (5) strengthened, because they remembered the poor.

> **BLESSED is he that considereth the poor: the LORD will DELIVER him in time of trouble.**
>
> **The LORD will PRESERVE him, and KEEP HIM ALIVE; and he shall be BLESSED upon the earth: and thou wilt not deliver him unto the will of his enemies.**
>
> **The LORD will STRENGTHEN him upon the bed of languishing: thou wilt make all his bed in his sickness.**
>
> **Psalm 41:1-3**

Who wouldn't want these blessings on his ministry? No wonder Cornelius received one of the most precious outpourings of the Holy Spirit recorded in the Bible.

Step 3: Pray

> **...and prayed to God alway...Thy prayers and thine alms are come up for a memorial before God.**
>
> **Acts 10:2, 4**

The next step to Cornelius' anointing was prayer. Scripture tells us how Cornelius' prayers attracted God's attention. Prayer has always been a key to the anointing. No one comes into the presence of God without praying.

One of the only prayer topics Jesus taught us to pray was to pray for the Holy Spirit.

If ye then, being evil, know how to give good gifts unto your children: how much more shall your heavenly Father give the Holy Spirit to them that ask him?

Luke 11:13

If you desire to be anointed, pray specifically for the coming of the anointing. Ask God to give you the Holy Spirit. Ask God to bless your ministry with His presence and power.

Keep praying the same thing for years and your prayers and alms will come up before God and arrest His attention. He will send an angel to you to guide you and bring you to the place of the anointing.

Step 4: Obey Visions

And when the angel which spake unto Cornelius was departed, he called two of his household servants, and a devout soldier of them that waited on him continually;

And when he had declared all these things unto them, he sent them to Joppa.

Acts 10:7-8

The next step to the anointing is to obey heavenly visions and dreams. Most of us have dreams and visions, which we do not obey. If we were to obey the visions and dreams that God gave us, we would experience the anointing. I know that your dreams seem vague and hazy. You think to yourself, surely, the visions and dreams of world-famous anointed men of God must have been clearer. I tell you, we all have vague and unclear dreams and visions from the Lord. The drive to obey these visions is the drive towards the anointing.

I cannot but thank God for the dreams and visions He has given me, no matter how vague they are. I would not be writing this book if I did not obey my visions and dreams. You will become anointed as you obey the visions and dreams that God gives you.

Each vision and each dream will take you one step closer on the journey to the anointing. Cornelius obeyed the vision and encountered the apostle Peter. Peter also obeyed a vision and met with Cornelius. This opened a door for Peter to preach to Cornelius. Whilst Peter was preaching, Cornelius and his entire household received the anointing. As you can see, one thing leads to another until you are standing in the river of the anointing.

Flow with your dreams! Flow with your visions! They are God's instruments encouraging you along the road to the anointing.

Step 5: Break Necessary Traditions

In order to be anointed, traditions had to be broken. Peter was not given to mixing with Gentiles. However, in order for the anointing of the Holy Spirit to be released, the lifestyle of Peter had to change.

> **And there came a voice to him, Rise, Peter; kill, and eat.**
> **But Peter said, Not so, Lord; for I have never eaten any thing that is common or unclean.**
> **And the voice spake unto him again the second time, What God hath cleansed, that call not thou common.**
> **Acts 10:13-15**

There are new things that God has in store for your life. People who cannot be guided into new things often do not receive the anointing.

Anointed people often wade into unchartered waters. Do you want God to use you? You may have to do some new things you have never done before. You may have to go to places you've never gone before.

Step 6: Obey the Man of God

Send therefore to Joppa, and call hither Simon, whose surname is Peter; he is lodged in the house of one Simon a tanner by the sea side: WHO, WHEN HE COMETH, SHALL SPEAK UNTO THEE.

Acts 10:32

And he commanded them...

Acts 10:48

The next step to Cornelius receiving the anointing was to be obedient to the instructions of the man of God. Just like dreams and visions, the commands of a man of God gently prod you further down the road to the anointing. One day, you will operate under a strong anointing and people will listen to you and obey your commands.

However, if you do not obey the instructions of the man of God, you are simply sowing the seeds of rebellion for your future.

Step 7: Listen to the Word of God

While Peter yet spake these words, the Holy Ghost fell on all them which heard the word.

Acts 10:44

Cornelius and his household were listening to the preaching of the Word of God when the Holy Ghost fell on them.

Ezekiel declared that the spirit entered into him when the Lord spoke to him.

And the spirit entered into me when he spake unto me, and set me upon my feet, that I heard him that spake unto me.

Ezekiel 2:2

Anyone who exposes himself to the preaching of the Word of God will become anointed. The Word of God is God! God is His Word and His Word is Him.

In the beginning was the Word and the Word was with God and the word was God.

John 1:1

The people in Cornelius' house were not prayed for. No one laid hands on them! No one touched them! No one blew wind on them! No one anointed them with oil! No one received an anointed prayer cloth! They were just listening to the anointed preaching of the Apostle Peter.

This is one of the greatest steps to the anointing and it is the step, which I experienced for myself in 1988 in a town called Suhum in Ghana.

God anointed me powerfully as I was listening to preaching by Kenneth Hagin. Since then, I have walked in the anointing and enjoyed God's power, and that is why you are reading this book.

Chapter 7

How to Persist until the Anointing Is Put to Use

Then shall the kingdom of heaven be likened unto ten virgins, which took their lamps, and went forth to meet the bridegroom. And five of them were wise, and five were foolish. They that were foolish took their lamps, and took no oil with them: But the wise took oil in their vessels with their lamps.

Matthew 25:1-4

Will you use the gift that God has placed in you? How sad it is that many talents are never used. In the famous parable of the ten virgins, only five of the virgins actually used their oil for the wedding. The other five virgins ended up going back home frustrated and unfulfilled. Many start out well but are not able to get to the place where the anointing can be used practically.

I remember sensing the call of God many years ago. I was a student and I would dream of preaching and teaching. This was a call of God being stirred up by the Holy Spirit. One day, it occurred to me whilst preaching that I had fulfilled a long-standing call.

Many people are called in their youth but miss the road that leads to practically using the anointing because they do not take the necessary steps. In this chapter, we will discuss how five out of ten virgins were able to persist in their calling until they actually used their gift.

Step 1: The Step of Virginity

Then shall the kingdom of heaven be likened unto ten virgins...

Matthew 25:1

In this story, only virgins carried the oil. Virginity is a sign of purity. Blessed are the pure in heart for they shall see God. It is the pure in heart who end up seeing the anointing and the power of the Holy Spirit. Virginity is a sign of purity that is not easy to see. The kind of purity that is needed to obtain the anointing is often difficult to see.

It is only God who sees the heart and judges accordingly. That is why people are often surprised at who God uses. They expect that God would use somebody else but God looks at the heart. Practise your Christianity before the Lord so that He is impressed. If He is pleased with you, you will receive the anointing.

Step 2: The Step of Phronimos

And five of them were wise (phronimos)...

Matthew 25:2

The virgins who used the anointing were described as wise virgins. The word "wise" comes from the Greek word "phronimos". This means to be sensible or practically wise. This kind of wisdom is different from the wisdom that makes you intelligent or clever. This word speaks of being sensible, level-headed, reasonable, and practical.

Many anointed people are not sensible or practical. Because of this lack of wisdom, many anointed men and women are not able to persist in ministry. Often, being sensible or practically wise makes you look unspiritual. It also has a way of making you look as though you have deviated from spiritual things. Yet, it is this practical wisdom that causes ministers to last longer.

Relaxing and resting often look like unspiritual, off-track activities. Taking your tablets everyday may not sound powerful or anointed, but it is sensible. Playing golf may look like a deviation from spiritual activity. Yet, it is this key that the five virgins had that enabled them to attend the wedding and use the anointing.

Wisdom is a key ingredient to arriving at the place where you use the anointing. Someone had a vision in which three angels, Faith, Hope and Love were battling on behalf of the saints. Faith, Hope, Love and the saints of God were losing the battle. Suddenly, a fourth angel appeared and that angel was Wisdom. As soon as the wisdom angel appeared, they began to win the battle.

This vision shows the importance of wisdom in our fight to serve the Lord. The absence of wisdom in your dealings can greatly set your ministry backwards. Financial problems, health problems, administrative problems and managerial problems will always hamper the anointing on your life. In the end, you will not be able to live long enough to practise all that you know and to use the anointing.

One day, I spoke to a young pastor who had begun a new, independent church. I sensed the presence of God and the anointing on his life. I also sensed that he was at an important crossroads which would make or break him. He would either go over or sink under. The key that would help him survive and persist so that the presence and unction in him would be put to the fullest use was the key of wisdom.

Oh, how I pray for wisdom! With wisdom, you can survive and stay out there longer. You can achieve what God has in store for you only through the key of wisdom.

Step 3: The Step of Knowing the Lord

But he answered and said, Verily I say unto you, I know you not.

Matthew 25:12

This is a very important step on the way to using the anointing. Without knowing God, you cannot survive. God is not a set of principles and neither is He a law book. He is Jehovah and you cannot go to Heaven without knowing Him. You cannot serve God with a "how to" book. You cannot go and live in someone's house if he does not know you. Why do you expect to live eternally in God's house when He does not know you and has no relationship with you?

Spend time seeking after the Lord. A daily quiet time, a daily personal time with the Father will change your life more than ten thousand church services which you attend.

Step 4: The Step of the Extra Mile

The wise, however, took oil in jars along with their lamps.

Matthew 25:4, NIV

The step of going the extra mile is a great key to actually fulfilling the call of God. Unfortunately, Christians do not know that the devil is going the extra mile to keep them out of the call of God. The devil is working overtime to deceive even the elect.

I have realized that Christians who don't go the extra mile for fellowship, soaking in the Word, prayer, and fasting, for example, do not amount to much in the ministry. Five of the virgins were ready to make the extra effort and to find some extra money to go the extra mile.

They made assurance double sure that they were going to be part of the wedding. The other five assumed that they would get in anyway. They took the ministry for granted and assumed that it would always be there for them. How wrong we can be!

The result of this tragic presumption was that they were left out of the glorious opportunity to partake in the wedding. May you not be left out of any spiritual impartation because you fail to pay the extra price necessary for the ministry!

Step 5: The Step of Tarrying

While the bridegroom tarried, they all slumbered and slept.

Matthew 25:5

Two types of tarrying are necessary for the anointing to become effective.

The first type of tarrying involves waiting for years until your time of fruitful ministry arrives. When the bridegroom tarried, all the virgins slept. There is nothing wrong with sleeping. What matters is to still be around when the right time comes. The five foolish virgins did not know that they would have to wait a long time to be able to use their gift.

Dear Christian friend, if you are not prepared to wait for several years for the right time, the right place and the right people, you will probably not amount to much. A certain level of ministry is realized only after many years. That is why it is important to start ministry early so you will be alive when that day comes.

The second type of tarrying involves praying and waiting on the Lord for hours. Without tarrying, you are simply not going to experience God's power and anointing. Tarrying takes up a central place on the road to practically using the anointing!

Step 6: The Step of Not Partaking in Other Men's Sins

And the foolish said unto the wise, Give us of your oil; for our lamps are gone out. But the wise answered, saying, Not so; lest there be not enough for us and you: but go ye rather to them that sell, and buy for yourselves.

Matthew 25:8-9

It is also important not to partake of other people's sins. Many people who are called will end up not fulfilling the call. Through laziness, sin and many other excuses, they will fail to do what they must do. Such people can easily take you along and drag you down with them.

The five wise virgins recognized that they were about to be drawn into a problem they did not have. They were about to become a part of a group to which they did not belong. They would soon be equally disqualified if they listened to these people.

It looked as though they were being asked to be "kind" and to "share" what they had but actually it was a temptation to forfeit their ministry. They said, "...not so, lest there be not enough for us and you."

Do not forsake your ministry for anyone. Neither your father, your mother, your husband nor your wife must be able to keep you from God's purpose. Children are no excuse to keep you from your calling. Don't join the people who have sacrificed their call for family, finances and comfort.

You are different! You have gone the extra mile. You ought to enter and fulfil your ministry for the glory of God.

Step 7: The Step of Ever-Readiness

And at midnight there was a cry made, Behold, the bridegroom cometh; go ye out to meet him. Then all those virgins arose, and trimmed their lamps.

Matthew 25:6-7

God can demand your life from you at anytime. God can also send you at any time. The bridegroom decided to have his wedding at midnight. This may sound unusual but that was what he decided to do.

You cannot tell God to call on you when you are ready. You cannot give God a time to call and check on you.

Sadly, this is what many of us do. You hear them say, "Wait till after my graduation." "Wait till after I get married!"

When you ask them to do the work of ministry they say, "Wait till after I get my new nationality."

"Wait till my children complete their school term, then we as a family, will be available."

"Wait until I pay for my house then I will apply for full-time ministry."

"Wait until I buy a new car."

"Wait until after my promotion; then I can serve God."

This is one reason why many people never practically use their mighty callings and gifts. They are just not ready at the time God calls on them. They wish God would call them at a more convenient time when they would have rounded up various things they are involved with. However, the bridegroom calls at midnight!

The bridegroom arrives later than expected and there is simply nothing you can do about it.

It is time to respond immediately! If you hear His voice, do not harden your heart!

Do not disrespect Him with your flimsy family excuses!

All those excuses simply abort your opportunity to use the oil! Remember that the devil is going the extra mile to prevent you from ever using that precious gift!

> **Watch therefore, for ye know neither the day nor the hour wherein the Son of man cometh.**
>
> **Matthew 25:13**

Chapter 8

Seven Steps to the Anointing in the Upper Room

But ye shall receive power, after that the Holy Ghost is come upon you: and ye shall be witnesses unto me both in Jerusalem, and in all Judaea, and in Samaria, and unto the uttermost part of the earth.

Acts 1:8

And they were all filled with the Holy Ghost, and began to speak with other tongues, as the Spirit gave them utterance.

Acts 2:4

Here stands the famous promise of our Lord Jesus Christ to send the power and anointing of the Holy Spirit to us! This chapter teaches about how to move from the promise of Acts 1:8 to its fulfilment in Acts 2:4; how to move from the hope of the anointing to the reality of actually experiencing the power of the Holy Ghost.

Step 1: Follow the Lord Faithfully for Several Years

Every single one of the people who received the anointing in the upper room had followed the Lord faithfully for several years. In choosing a replacement for Judas Iscariot, the apostles specified that it had to be someone who had been around for a long time.

Therefore it is necessary that of the men who have accompanied us all the time that the Lord Jesus went in and out among us – beginning with the baptism of John until the day that He was taken up from us

– one of these must become a witness with us of His resurrection. So they put forward two men...

Acts 1:21-23, NASB

The qualification for becoming an apostle was to have been around for at least three years. Do not expect to receive the most important treasures of God's kingdom after serving the Lord for a few minutes.

Step 2: Be Available to Experience Everything God Has for You

The people who received the anointing were those who had actually seen the risen Lord. For forty days, some people had the amazing experience of meeting with the resurrected Lord.

Definitely, the experience of seeing the resurrected Christ would have an impact on their spiritual lives.

To whom also he shewed himself alive after his passion by many infallible proofs, being seen of them forty days, and speaking of the things pertaining to the kingdom of God:

Acts 1:3

Those who missed this experience were obviously going to be different. There can be no experience that compares with meeting a resurrected person. This would have a profound effect on anyone.

All the different experiences God allows you to have, prepare you for the anointing! People you meet and know can change your life forever. The things you hear and experience are not by accident. They are part of the build-up towards the day when the power of the Spirit will be poured out on you.

The churches I attended, the pastors I knew and the people I met, were all divinely arranged to prepare me for my ministry. I believe this strongly. To a believer, there is no accident or coincidence to anything. God rules in the affairs of all men. Do not shy away from any work of the ministry. Do not miss the opportunities to be close to God's power.

Step 3: Decide Not to Follow Politics

Sadly, many people are distracted by politics and earthly power. The disciples fell for this common ministry trap. Following the Lord's resurrection, they felt that this great power would now be turned towards the achievement of earthly goals. The disciples were ready to fight for the political liberation of Israel from the Romans.

When they therefore were come together, they asked of him, saying, Lord, wilt thou at this time restore again the kingdom to Israel? And he said unto them, It is not for you to know the times or the seasons, which the Father hath put in his own power.

Acts 1:6-7

Having been in the ministry for some years, I can see how easy it is to be distracted from real, Holy Spirit ministry and into a humanistic gospel.

Step 4: Be a Humble Part of the Group to Which God Has Called You

Being part of your fellowship is one of the greatest steps towards the anointing. God has called us to be sheep that belong to a flock. It takes humility to stay a part of the group to which you belong. When you become a minister, you are still a sheep and you belong somewhere.

And, being assembled together with them, commanded them that they should not depart from Jerusalem...

Acts 1:4

Continuing to assemble together with the fellowship that God has given you, will eventually lead you to the anointing. Do not abandon your fellowship. Do not desert your brothers and your friends.

Through your participation in this group, you shall be anointed. I can point to several levels of the anointing that I experienced because I was a part of a fellowship. God's power will come to you through the group He has appointed you to.

Step 5: Follow the Wisdom and the Direction of the Lord

...commanded them that they should not depart from Jerusalem...

Acts 1:4

The ministry belongs to the Lord. It is His church. He said, "I will build my church." To become anointed, you need to follow the directives of Jesus.

If the disciples had not waited in Jerusalem, they would not have received the anointing. Only those who were in Jerusalem on the day of Pentecost received the Holy Spirit.

If you learn to follow the direction of the Holy Spirit, you will become anointed! One thing leads to another. Often, we do not know the far-reaching implications of the commands of the Lord.

Step 6: Wait on God

...but wait for the promise of the Father, which, saith he, ye have heard of me.

Acts 1:4

Waiting on God is an important step to becoming anointed! As you wait on the Lord, you will become anointed. Isaiah's prophecy contains an ancient Jewish promise about the power of waiting on the Lord.

Yet those who wait for the LORD Will gain new strength; They will mount up with wings like eagles, They will run and not get tired, They will walk and not become weary.

Isaiah 40:31, NASB

Right here is a promise for strength and for soaring up in ministry. There is also a promise for running and walking in the ministry without becoming weary. Men of God do not get tired because of the anointing.

Unfortunately, few Christians have the time to wait on the Lord. They therefore leave out of their lives one of the most powerful keys for becoming anointed.

Step 7: Love and Unity

And when the day of Pentecost was fully come, they were all with one accord in one place.

Acts 2:1

If you want to experience the anointing, you will have to move away from strife, confusion, and bitterness. Your ministry team will need to be of one mind and one heart. God does not anoint a confused quarrelling mob, which is rife with competition and politics.

You will notice that the apostles had to wait until they were all in one place and with one accord before the anointing came upon them. You will not find the anointing in a team, which is filled with bitterness and hatred. You will always find the anointing where there is unity.

a.   Solomon experienced the glory and the anointing in his new temple when all the musicians and singers were united and of one accord.

It came even to pass, as the trumpeters and singers were as one, to make one sound to be heard in praising and thanking the LORD; and when they lifted up their

voice with the trumpets and cymbals and instruments of musick, and praised the LORD, saying, For he is good; for his mercy endureth for ever: that then the house was filled with a cloud, even the house of the LORD;

So that the priests could not stand to minister by reason of the cloud: for the glory of the LORD had filled the house of God.

2 Chronicles 5:13-14

b. King David, the anointed psalmist, sang about the beauty of unity and how it attracted the anointing.

Behold, how good and how pleasant it is for brothers to dwell together in unity!

It is like the precious oil upon the head...

Psalm 133:1-2

c. The apostle Paul warned that all fellowship and anointing of the Spirit would be experienced through unity.

Therefore if there is any encouragement in Christ, if there is any consolation of love, if there is any fellowship of the Spirit, if any affection and compassion, make my joy complete by being of the same mind, maintaining the same love, united in spirit, intent on one purpose. Do nothing from selfishness or empty conceit, but with humility of mind regard one another as more important than yourselves;

Philippians 2:1-3, NASB

Chapter 9

Seven Steps to the Anointing in Your Own Company

And being let go, they went to their own company, and reported all that the chief priests and elders had said unto them. And when they heard that, they lifted up their voice to God with one accord, and said, Lord, thou art God, which hast made heaven, and earth, and the sea, and all that in them is: Who by the mouth of thy servant David hast said, Why did the heathen rage, and the people imagine vain things?

The kings of the earth stood up, and the rulers were gathered together against the Lord, and against his Christ. For of a truth against thy holy child Jesus, whom thou hast anointed, both Herod, and Pontius Pilate, with the Gentiles, and the people of Israel, were gathered together, For to do whatsoever thy hand and thy counsel determined before to be done.

And now, Lord, behold their threatenings: and grant unto thy servants, that with all boldness they may speak thy word, By stretching forth thine hand to heal; and that signs and wonders may be done by the name of thy holy child Jesus. And when they had prayed, the place was shaken where they were assembled together; and they were all filled with the Holy Ghost, and they spake the word of God with boldness.

Acts 4:23-31

Step 1: Know and Believe that You Can Be Anointed Again and Again

It is obvious from the text that Peter, John and many of the other disciples were present for two of the recorded anointings of the Holy Spirit in the book of Acts. This means that they received

51

the Holy Spirit twice. They were filled twice. They were anointed twice. They received the Holy Spirit repeatedly. The first anointing of the Holy Spirit was recorded in Acts chapter two and the second in Acts chapter four.

And they were all filled with the Holy Ghost, and began to speak with other tongues, as the Spirit gave them utterance.

Acts 2:4

And when they had prayed, the place was shaken where they were assembled together; and they were all filled with the Holy Ghost, and they spake the word of God with boldness.

Acts 4:31

It is important to believe that you can be anointed many times. Recently, the Lord impressed on me that there are many gifts and anointings available for His servants.

Somehow, there is a feeling that there are only five main gifts of ministry which work with nine subsidiary gifts. Also, there is a feeling that there is one baptism of the Holy Spirit after which we have finished with the Holy Spirit.

These two thoughts are delusions that keep us from further anointings and gifts of the Holy Spirit. You can be anointed many times and you must expect many gifts. At different times and seasons of your life, God will give you the anointings that you need.

There is not just one anointing. There are several measures of anointing that you will have before it is all over. Jesus is the only One who had the anointing without measure.

Step 2: Embrace Persecution Because It Brings out the Anointing

Who by the mouth of thy servant David hast said, Why did the heathen rage, and the people imagine vain

things? The kings of the earth stood up, and the rulers were gathered together against the Lord, and against his Christ.

Acts 4:25-26

The disciples experienced persecution. Persecution makes you either bitter or better. It brings out the best in you or the worst in you. Out of the thousands that experienced the wilderness, only Joshua and Caleb emerged with a good attitude.

Jesus was tempted in the wilderness for forty days and nights. He came out shining and ready to flow in the power of the Holy Spirit.

The Lord does not tempt us but He does test us. The Scripture unambiguously teaches us that God leads us through the wilderness to see what is in our hearts.

And thou shalt remember all the way which the LORD thy God led thee these forty years in the wilderness, to humble thee, and to prove thee, to know what was in thine heart, whether thou wouldest keep his commandments, or no.

Deuteronomy 8:2

Persecution will make you either bitter or better. Let your troubles lead you to trust in the Lord and in His power and anointing.

Step 3: Obey God in Spite of the Pressure You Have from Men

For we cannot but speak the things which we have seen and heard.

Acts 4:20

Become like Peter and John who would rather obey God than men.

But Peter and John answered and said unto them, Whether it be right in the sight of God to hearken unto you more than unto God, judge ye.

Acts 4:19

This is a crucial step towards the anointing. Obey God in spite of the pressure you have from men. When you stop yielding to the pressure that comes from human beings, you will discover the anointing. Much of ministry involves going opposite to the way people want you to go.

Step 4: Do Not Be Moved by Threats, Accusations and Other Forms of Intimidation

So when they had further threatened them, they let them go...

Acts 4:21

If threats and accusations can move you from your calling, then you are not worthy of the anointing. As you serve the Lord, there will be threats, constant accusations, and much intimidation. It is part of the package to be harassed by accusers! Your motives will be challenged continually! It takes strength to continue walking steadily towards your goal, in spite of insinuations, suspicions and annoying accusations.

Step 5: Have Your Own Company to Which You Belong

And being let go, they went to their own company...

Acts 4:23

When they were let go they went to their own company. It is important to have your own company who believe in you and who can accommodate you as you really are. Your own company is the small group or fellowship to which you belong.

They are your brothers and sisters in the Lord. They are your colleagues in the ministry. They are your friends with whom you will live and die. You will be buried together with your own company and rise with them at the resurrection.

Seven Advantages of Having Your Own Company

a.   Your own company will believe in you when no one else does.

b.   Your own company will help you when no one else will.

c.   Your own company will accommodate your weaknesses when no one else will.

d.   Your own company will like you as you are.

e.   Your own company will welcome you when no other group is happy to see you.

f.   Your own company will cover up for you when you fall into their hands.

g.   Your own company will lift you up when you make a mistake.

Step 6: Pray Specifically for Power, Miracles, Signs and Wonders

This group, which received the anointing, prayed fervently for miracles, signs and wonders. They prayed specifically for signs and wonders to be done at the hands of the apostles. It may interest you to know that God does listen to specific requests that we make. They prayed for healings, they prayed for signs and wonders and they prayed for God's outstretched hand.

And when they heard that, they lifted up their voice to God with one accord, and said... By stretching forth thine hand to heal; and that signs and wonders may be done by the name of thy holy child Jesus.

And when they had prayed, the place was shaken where they were assembled together...

Acts 4:24, 30-31

What a powerful prayer! Someone said he prayed for twenty-five years to receive visions and dreams. After twenty-five years, he began to have some of the most amazing visions, which have blessed many people. Do not minimize the importance of your powerful prayers. Pray for the anointing. Pray for miracles. Pray for healing. They will be yours in the name of Jesus.

Step 7: United Prayer

...they lifted up their voice to God with one accord...

Acts 4:24

We are truly blessed when we wait on God. However, great power is released when you pray together with others who have the same mind and heart. Jesus had two kinds of prayer times. At times, He prayed all alone and at times, He prayed with His disciples.

Praying with Others

When you pray together with brothers and friends who have the same attitude towards ministry, you accomplish much in the Spirit. This is the kind of prayer that the prophets and teachers practised in the thirteenth chapter of Acts. It is this group prayer which led to the apostolic ministry of Paul and Barnabas.

> **Now there were in the church that was at Antioch certain prophets and teachers; as Barnabas, and Simeon that was called Niger, and Lucius of Cyrene, and Manaen, which had been brought up with Herod the tetrarch, and Saul.**

> **As they ministered to the Lord, and fasted, the Holy Ghost said, Separate me Barnabas and Saul for the work whereunto I have called them.**

And when they had fasted and prayed, and laid their hands on them, they sent them away.

Acts 13:1-3

Praying Alone

Another way is to spend long hours alone with God. This is what happened when Moses went up into the mountain all alone to wait on the Lord.

And the LORD said unto Moses, Come up to me into the mount, and be there: and I will give thee tables of stone, and a law, and commandments which I have written; that thou mayest teach them.

Exodus 24:12

Chapter 10

Steps to the Anointing in the Holy Hill

LORD, who shall abide in thy tabernacle? who shall dwell in thy holy hill? He that walketh uprightly, and worketh righteousness, and speaketh the truth in his heart. He that backbiteth not with his tongue, nor doeth evil to his neighbour, nor taketh up a reproach against his neighbour. In whose eyes a vile person is contemned; but he honoureth them that fear the LORD. He that sweareth to his own hurt, and changeth not. He that putteth not out his money to usury, nor taketh reward against the innocent. He that doeth these things shall never be moved.

Psalm 15

In the book of Psalms, the dwelling place of God is often described as "the holy hill".

David often sang about going up to the holy hill where God dwelt. The anointed psalmist had visions of himself ascending into God's habitation. His dream was to "dwell in the house of the Lord forever."

David also knew that not everyone could come into that holy place. He knew that help and answers for prayer would come from this holy hill.

I cried unto the LORD with my voice, and he heard me out of his holy hill...

Psalm 3:4

Even in the natural, not everyone comes into the king's palace. Few people ever see the inside of royal palaces. It is a common sight to see thousands of tourists standing outside the Buckingham palace gazing longingly at the building. I have done so myself.

I wondered, "Where exactly does the Queen live? What are their rooms like? What do they eat in the palace? Do they have special sausages and special bread made for them?"

We all know that it would be a privilege to even peep into one of these royal rooms.

Who shall ascend into the hill of the LORD? or who shall stand in his holy place?

Psalm 24:3

Who amongst us will be privileged to ascend into the holy hill where God dwells. Which of us will enjoy His presence and His power in our lives? We can only have that great power if we can come near to where God dwells. Here are sixteen steps that lead to the holy hill.

Step 1: Walk uprightly.

To approach the place of the anointing, you need to be a person who is upright and straightforward.

He that walketh uprightly...

Psalm 15:2

Step 2: Work righteousness.

The second step to the anointing is to be a doer of works of righteousness. Give yourself to doing the works of God and the good deeds that God has determined for you.

...and worketh righteousness...

Psalm 15:2

Step 3: Speak the truth in your heart.

The third step is all about speaking the truth. Speaking the truth in your heart is all about being honest and telling yourself the truth.

...and speaketh the truth in his heart.

Psalm 15:2

Step 4: Do not backbite with your tongue.

This next step to the anointing is to keep your tongue from speaking evil. Death and life are in the power of the tongue. You can let your tongue bring you into a place of anointing or you can let your tongue destroy your ministry.

He that backbiteth not with his tongue...

Psalm 15:3

Step 5: Do not do evil to your neighbour.

The next step to the anointing is to be good to people who are near to you (your neighbours). Doing evil to people who are close to you is a dangerous sign.

...nor doeth evil to his neighbour...

Psalm 15:3

Watch out and make sure you do not do evil to your neighbour - to your husband, your wife, your brothers or your sisters.

Step 6: Do not accuse your neighbour.

An anointed person is not an accuser. Train yourself to intercede and to have eyes of love and understanding.

...nor taketh up a reproach against his neighbour.

Psalm 15:3

Step 7: Do not admire evil doers.

Do not admire rebels and evil doers. What you admire speaks volumes about who you are.

In whose eyes a reprobate is despised...

Psalm 15:4

You must despise what God despises and love what God loves.

Step 8: Honour those who fear God.

The eighth step to the anointing is to honour people who love God. This means to honour and love all people who serve God, even if they are not in your denomination. You must even love the faithful ones who serve God in smallness and simplicity.

When God detects that your heart is bigger than your little group, then you are ready for the anointing.

...but he honoureth them that fear the Lord...

Psalm 15:4

It's time to see the good in the many different groups of people that love God. Since God revealed this to me, I have found myself admiring all kinds of people whom I had previously despised. The people to be despised are reprobates and not those who fear God!

Step 9: Keep your promises.

...He that sweareth to his own hurt, and changeth not.

Psalm 15:4

Keeping to your word is very important. You need to be a man whose words mean something. God is looking for people who do what they say they will do.

When you are a man of your word, you will be ready for the anointing. God has no time for fools whose words mean nothing. You may continue to be a member of the church, but if you want to carry the precious anointing you may need to become a man whose words and promises are kept.

Step 10: Do not cheat innocent people.

When you become anointed, you will be a man with much authority. If you misuse this authority you will hurt a lot of people. Your wickedness will result in much suffering for many people.

He that putteth not out his money to usury nor taketh reward against the innocent...

Psalm 15:5

You must become someone who does not take advantage of innocent and poor people.

The earth is the LORD's, and the fulness thereof; the world, and they that dwell therein.

For he hath founded it upon the seas, and established it upon the floods.

Who shall ascend into the hill of the LORD? or who shall stand in his holy place?

He that hath clean hands, and a pure heart; who hath not lifted up his soul unto vanity, nor sworn deceitfully.

Psalm 24:1-4

Step 11: Have clean hands.

He that hath clean hands...

Psalm 24:4

To have clean hands speaks of guiltlessness in the secret places. When your hands are clean it means you have not engaged in certain sins. When you are anointed, God will use your hands to touch many lives.

Step 12: Have a pure heart.

...and a pure heart...

Psalm 24:4

It is also important to have a pure heart if you are going to be anointed. God deals with the heart and not with the outward things that human beings see. David was anointed because of the kind of heart he had.

Unfortunately, most people look on the outward appearance. Even an experienced prophet like Samuel was mistaken when he looked on the outward appearance. Work on your heart because that is what God looks at. Do not feel secure because people praise you. What people think is often wrong. It is what God thinks and says that matters.

Step 13: Avoid vanity.

...who hath not lifted up his soul unto vanity...

Psalm 24:4

An anointed person cannot engage in frivolous and inconsequential activities. There are many useless time-wasting activities that an anointed person cannot be involved with.

Remove useless socializing from your life. Within the ministry, you must treasure things that have eternal value and that God Himself desires. You cannot lift your soul up into vanity.

Step 14: Do not swear deceitfully.

...nor sworn deceitfully.

Psalm 24:4

Making useless promises is a sure step away from the anointing. An anointed person has to keep his word. He cannot deceive with his words. He is a proclaimer of God's Word and God's purpose.

Step 15: Seek the Lord.

This is the generation of them that seek him, that seek thy face, O Jacob.

Psalm 24:6

Seeking the Lord and waiting on Him is a sure way to approach the anointing. He that waits on the Lord will surely renew his strength.

Step 16: Follow the light and truth of God's Word.

> **O send out THY LIGHT AND THY TRUTH: LET THEM LEAD ME; let them bring me unto thy holy hill, and to thy tabernacles.**
>
> **Then will I go unto the altar of God, unto God my exceeding joy: yea, upon the harp will I praise thee, O God my God.**
>
> Psalm 43:3-4

As you follow the light of God's Word, you will come into a place of anointing. The light and truth of God's Word brings you to the presence of God.

Chapter 11

Seven Steps to an Anointing You Can Feel

The woman with the issue of blood had a common gynaecological disorder and was desperately in need of a miracle. Her testimony is one of the most powerful illustrations of how a person can receive an anointing. It is a very important testimony because it illustrates:

a. How healings actually take place: healings take place when the healing anointing leaves the man of God and moves into the one who is healed.

b. The role of feelings in the ministry of the Spirit: we learn from this story that the anointing can be felt. "I am not moved by what I see, I am not moved by what I feel" is a nice song and is true in many ways. However, this testimony reveals that there is a place for feeling the anointing.

c. We also see how a person ministering can sometimes feel the anointing moving from him.

d. We learn how a person receiving a miracle may actually feel when it is happening.

e. Finally, we discover the revelation of more steps to receiving the anointing.

Seven Steps to Receiving the Anointing

Step 1: Endure your appointed suffering.

And a certain woman, which had an issue of blood twelve years, And had suffered many things of many physicians, and had spent all that she had, and was nothing bettered, but rather grew worse,

Mark 5:25-26

In order to receive the anointing, you will have to suffer certain things. This woman sought after Christ because she suffered from a chronic illness; she had an unsolvable condition. The kingdom of God is not about what you know or who your parents are. It's about what you have been through, what you have suffered and what you have survived!!

Contrary to what is taught by the church today, we are actually appointed and ordained to suffer certain things.

And sent Timotheus, our brother, and minister of God, and our fellowlabourer in the gospel of Christ, to establish you, and to comfort you concerning your faith:

That no man should be moved by these afflictions: for yourselves know that we are appointed thereunto.

1 Thessalonians 3:2-3

At Paul's conversion, a prophet was sent to show him how much he must suffer.

But the Lord said unto him, Go thy way: for he is a chosen vessel unto me...For I will shew him how great things he must suffer for my name's sake.

Acts 9:15-16

Paul's calling to the high office of apostle was a calling to suffer. It was a calling to experience hardships and difficulties. Somehow, suffering softens you, humbles you, and enables you to receive the anointing. Pride cannot receive from God; pride causes God to dislike you and resist you. Many times, in order to get rid of the pride, God will take you to a humbling place.

Step 2: Wait for your time.

And a certain woman, which had an issue of blood twelve years,

Mark 5:25

God had determined that this woman would receive the anointing only after twelve years of suffering; she encountered Jesus only after she had suffered for twelve long years. There is a time for everything, including a time to be anointed (Ecclesiastes 3:1). You must wait for the time of the anointing.

Often, people who experience a certain level of the anointing have suffered for many years. What have you been through? What have you suffered? What have you survived?

Step 3: Hear the right things.

   When she had heard of Jesus...

Mark 5:27

Perhaps one of the important steps to the anointing is hearing the right things. You will be ushered into all that God has for you through what you hear. Faith simply comes by hearing. If you hear about the anointing, you will believe in it and you will expect it. If you hear about visions and revelations you will expect them. Every minister is limited by what he hears.

Expose yourself to the right preaching and teaching and you will come into a place of anointing. I received the anointing as I was listening to anointed preaching by Kenneth Hagin.

Step 4: Go to the anointed for his anointing.

   When she...came in the press behind...

Mark 5:27

This woman went to seek Jesus to receive the anointing for healing. Sometimes you have to physically go to a place so that you can be anointed. You may have to travel to another country in order to come in contact with the anointed man and his anointing. Do anything you need to in order to encounter anointed people.

There are some people who are carrying a mantle that God has determined to give to you. They are actually in possession of an anointing that is yours. Elijah carried Elisha's anointing for years and it was up to Elisha to get it. Elisha had to leave his oxen and live with the anointed man in order to get his anointing.

Step 5: Say the right things.

For she said, If I may touch but his clothes, I shall be whole.

Mark 5:28

Death and life are in the power of the tongue. What you say will greatly affect everything about your life and future. Even your jokes can affect you. Receiving or losing the anointing is associated with what you say.

The Syrophenician woman received the healing anointing for her child because of what she said. Jesus told her why she was going to receive the power of God - because of what she said.

For a certain woman, whose young daughter had an unclean spirit, heard of him, and came and fell at his feet: The woman was a Greek, a Syrophenician by nation; and she besought him that he would cast forth the devil out of her daughter.

But Jesus said unto her, Let the children first be filled: for it is not meet to take the children's bread, and to cast it unto the dogs. And she answered and said unto him, Yes, Lord: yet the dogs under the table eat of the children's crumbs. And he said unto her,

For this saying go thy way; the devil is gone out of thy daughter.

Mark 7:25-29

Step 6: Understand how the anointing is carried and transmitted.

For she said, If I may touch but his clothes, I shall be whole.

Mark 5:28

The anointing is often carried by wind, oil, cloth, garments, etc. (See my book, *"Amplify Your Ministry with Miracles and Manifestations of the Holy Spirit*). It is important to understand these realities if you are to receive the anointing. Coming into contact with these things can actually cause you to be anointed.

In this case, the woman believed that she would receive the anointing through a cloth. She believed that there was power in the garments of an anointed person. Perhaps her Jewish background caused her to understand and believe this reality even more. She had seen how the priests' garments were anointed. She had heard of the anointing being carried by the mantle of the anointed man. The garments of priests were anointed in the Old Testament. This showed that the anointing was to be carried in the clothes of the priests.

And Moses took of the anointing oil, and of the blood which was upon the altar, and sprinkled it upon Aaron, and upon his garments, and upon his sons, and upon his sons' garments with him; and sanctified Aaron, and his garments, and his sons, and his sons' garments with him

Leviticus 8:30

Handkerchiefs and aprons were taken from the body of Paul. These cloths carried the anointing and were able to drive out diseases.

So that from his body were brought unto the sick handkerchiefs or aprons, and the diseases departed from them, and the evil spirits went out of them.

Acts 19:12

The mantle of Elijah (another type of cloth) carried the anointing. That is why Elijah threw it onto Elisha when he called him into the ministry. That is why Elisha picked it up after Elijah was taken up to Heaven. He used it as a tool of the anointing to strike the river Jordan and to part it.

Saul recognized the prophet Samuel by his mantle. Saul asked the witch to describe the man she saw. When she said he had a mantle on, Saul knew it had to be the prophet.

And he said unto her, What form is he of? And she said, An old man cometh up; and he is covered with a mantle. And Saul perceived that it was Samuel, and he stooped with his face to the ground, and bowed himself.

1 Samuel 28:14

The garments of Jesus were anointed. That is why the woman with the issue of blood had only to touch the hem of His garment in order for her to be healed.

Step 7: Be a daughter.

And he said unto her, Daughter, thy faith hath made thee whole; go in peace, and be whole of thy plague.

Mark 5:34

Jesus could have referred to her and said, "Woman, thy faith hath made thee whole." But He called her "daughter". There is a difference between a woman and a daughter. A daughter is a trusting, humble and childlike person.

Be childlike. Be humble and you will have access to all the gifts of the kingdom. The key that opens all the doors to all the rooms of the anointing is humility. Perhaps that is why you have not received the anointing. You need to be childlike and trusting in relation to the anointed and his anointing. A lot of analysis and critique will not bring you into a place of anointing.

Chapter 12

The Anointing of Prophets and Righteous Men

...many prophets and righteous men have desired to see those things...

Matthew 13:17

Jesus was the anointing that many prophets and righteous men had desired to see. He was the great anointing expected for centuries by the Jews. He was called Christ, the Anointed One.

Yet, the people could not receive from this great gift. What is it that kept them from the power that was walking around in Jerusalem? What was it that blinded their eyes from seeing the anointing when it was right in front of them?

Here was the anointing that many prophets and righteous men had hoped for and they could neither recognize nor receive it. Is it possible that there are great anointings near us that we are neither able to recognize nor receive?

In this chapter, I am going to share with you seven steps that Jesus spoke about. These steps would have caused the people of His day to experience that great anointing.

These same steps will lead you to receive powerful gifts and anointings that God has for you. There is no point in having great anointings near you and not being able to access them.

You can be anointed! You can receive it too. God's will shall be done and the anointing will come through to you!

These seven steps begin with Jesus explaining how God sovereignly chooses who is to receive of the mysteries of God and end when conversion and healing come to the soul.

Step 1: To Be Divinely Chosen for the Anointing

… it is given unto you to know the mysteries of the kingdom of heaven, but to them it is not given.

Matthew 13:11

It is important to recognize that the anointing is a divine gift. Inasmuch as we are sharing some steps to receiving this anointing, it is not something anyone can just work up. It is God's choice to give you the anointing or not.

Step 2: To Have Some Anointing

For whosoever hath, to him shall be given, and he shall have more abundance: but whosoever hath not, from him shall be taken away even that he hath.

Matthew 13:12

One of the most encouraging realities is to know that if you already have some anointing, you become a candidate to receive even more. Over and over in the Scripture, it is shown that if you have some gift you are a candidate for more.

If you perceive that God has given you a gift, please open your heart to receive more because that is the law of the kingdom. This must be very encouraging to anyone who is in the ministry.

If you are a pastor, you could receive a higher anointing for a greater ministry. If you have dreams and visions, you are more likely to receive even greater revelations. So press on and expect more power to be available to you.

Step 3: To Be Able to See What You Must See

But blessed are your eyes, for they see: and your ears, for they hear.

Matthew 13:16

The third step to the anointing is to have eyes that can see. Sometimes, I would ask, "Did you see Sister Comfort?" and the answer would be, "Was she the one with long curly hair in the red and mauve silk scarf?"

And I would say, "What was that?"

I surely saw Sister Comfort but I would not remember what hair she had nor whether she had a scarf on.

You see, everybody's eyes see different things. When someone stands to minister, some people see a doctor ministering. Others see a tall, dark preacher. Others see an unmarried man and a potential husband. Still others see an educated person in action. But, very few people see what they should really see.

It is important to see and recognize the anointing when it is at work.

One day, I encouraged a sister to serve God in full-time ministry.

After talking to her for hours, she stared at me blandly and remarked, "Pastor, my family does not have as much money as yours."

"I am not like you," she said. "If I do not work in the secular world, I will not be able to survive." I was taken aback. I realized that all this lady could see was my father's wealth. She could not see the anointing or the grace of God at work. Unfortunately, her inability to see God's power and not my father's money prevented her from coming towards the anointing.

Perhaps this is the greatest blockade to receiving the anointing. When you see someone, there is often an aspect of the person that your eyes settle on. You may see his wealth, his background, his education, his kindness, his wisdom, his love, his car, his house, and the list goes on. Some people only look at his wife. Some only analyze the kind of person he has married.

One Sunday, one of my pastors introduced me to his church. Somehow, I always remember that particular introduction. He introduced me as an anointed person! He said he had realized that there was a very strong anointing on my life that supernaturally affected people.

He spoke about how the anointing on me had supernaturally affected him. He did not speak about how many churches I had built nor how many sermons I had preached. He did not say where he met me or how kind I was. He just spoke about the anointing and I realized that his eyes were trained on something invisible that was both spiritual and eternal.

What you see will greatly determine what you will ultimately receive.

Step 4: To Be Able to Hear What You Must Hear

...their ears are dull of hearing, and their eyes they have closed...

Matthew 13:15

Once again, as people listen to you they all hear different things. The first thing most people hear is your accent. If it is the wrong accent, they will not hear the powerful words of life that you speak.

Others only hear the correctness of the grammar and your choice of words. Some people hear the stories that you tell and others remember only the jokes! Still others hear the principles and the Scriptures that you share. And yet, there are some who hear things that are beyond any of these.

They hear the Spirit speaking! They receive wisdom from the Holy Spirit! Some receive life changing guidance from the Holy Spirit! Somehow, everybody hears differently! Jesus knew that people were hearing differently and that is why He said, "... Hearing they cannot hear." May your ears hear what they must hear! If you begin to hear correctly, you will come closer to the anointing that prophets and anointed men desire.

Step 5: To Be Able to Understand

...and shall not understand; and seeing ye shall see, and shall not perceive:

Matthew 13:14

Many people have difficulty in understanding issues. This becomes a great barrier to receiving anything. Such people cannot have a peaceful marriage. They never understand issues, no matter how it is explained and how many illustrations are used.

There is no point counselling such people as their minds are made up already. The Scripture is clear, "...with all thy getting get understanding" (Proverbs 4:7). Understanding what is being said is crucial to the anointing passing through the barrier of your mind and entering your spirit.

When you lack understanding, your mind forms a blockade that cuts out the Word of God and all its attendant blessings.

How difficult it is to be married to someone who does not understand issues. This person (man or woman) never agrees to anything, never says yes, never says no, never bends, never yields, never gives in, never sees the point, never flows, and ultimately never understands!!

May God touch your understanding that you may see and know the greatness of the anointing that is near you.

Step 6: To Understand with the Heart

...and should understand with their heart...

Matthew 13:15

There is yet a higher level of understanding. This is the place of understanding issues with the heart. When a person understands with his heart, there is no need for extensive explanation. To understand with the heart means to have a depth of revelation that takes away the need for numerous discussions, meetings, demonstrations of data and statistical analysis.

When someone understands with the heart, at the beginning of the discussion, he would say something like, "I understand." "Don't bother to explain." "I will sort it out." "Just leave it to me."

What a blessing it is to have people who understand with the heart.

Many times, the man of God cannot explain everything that is going on. He may not even be able to describe everything that he is feeling. He needs people who are in tune with him and who understand with their hearts.

When you begin to understand God with your heart, you are getting nearer to your conversion, your healing and your anointing!

Step 7: To Be Converted

For this people's heart is waxed gross, and their ears are dull of hearing, and their eyes they have closed; lest at any time they should see with their eyes, and hear with their ears, and should understand with their heart, AND SHOULD BE CONVERTED, AND I SHOULD HEAL THEM.

Matthew 13:15

The final step towards the anointing that even prophets and righteous men desire is to be converted (to change).

Ultimately, God is changing us into His image. Everyone who becomes anointed has been worked upon and has undergone various "conversions".

The Scripture above shows that a change is required before the healing "anointing" comes. Much change is required to carry the grace of God. The vessel must change! Your life must be completely transformed if you are to receive the anointing.

Chapter 13

Restrictions for the Anointed

The restrictions placed on an anointed priest give us great insight into the restrictions that pertain to a truly anointed person.

Under the old covenant, anointed priests had some restrictions. These old covenant restrictions teach us about restrictions that anointed men of God have on their lives today.

Moses gave these restrictions to Aaron and the other priests. He explained that these restrictions were because of the anointing oil that was poured on them! There were no other reasons for the restrictions but the fact that the anointing oil had been poured on them. You see, when a person is anointed, he is sanctified by the anointing.

Thou shalt sanctify him therefore; for he offereth the bread of thy God: he shall be holy...

Leviticus 21:8

To be sanctified means that you are now a special person, reserved and separated for God's service. In a sense, you are married to God's house. You are not free anymore and cannot do just whatever you want. What a small price to pay for the privilege of being an anointed person.

Why There Are Restrictions on Anointed People

1.   Anointed people are sanctified by the anointing.

And Moses took of the anointing oil, and of the blood which was upon the altar, and sprinkled it upon Aaron, and upon his garments, and upon his sons, and upon his sons' garments with him; AND SANCTIFIED

AARON, AND HIS GARMENTS, AND HIS SONS, and his sons' garments with him.

Leviticus 8:30

2.   The work of the ministry is restricted to sanctified people.

Then Moses said unto Aaron, This is it that the LORD spake, saying, I WILL BE SANCTIFIED IN THEM THAT COME NIGH ME, and before all the people I will be glorified. And Aaron held his peace.

Leviticus 10:3

3.   To be sanctified is to be separated and made specially holy for service.

Thou shalt sanctify him therefore; for he offereth the bread of thy God: he shall be holy unto thee: for I the LORD, which sanctify you, am holy.

Leviticus 21:8

And thou shalt put them upon Aaron thy brother, and his sons with him; and shalt anoint them, and consecrate them, and sanctify them, that they may minister unto me in the priest's office.

Exodus 28:41

4.   Sanctified (separated and holy) people are therefore restricted people.

And ye shall not go out from the door of the tabernacle of the congregation, lest ye die: for the anointing oil of the LORD is upon you. And they did according to the word of Moses.

Leviticus 10:7

NEITHER SHALL HE GO OUT of the sanctuary, nor profane the sanctuary of his God; FOR THE CROWN

OF THE ANOINTING OIL OF HIS GOD IS UPON HIM: I am the LORD.

Leviticus 21:12

5.   It is dangerous to violate the restrictions on the anointing.

And there went out fire from the LORD, and devoured them, and they died before the LORD. Then Moses said unto Aaron, This is it that the LORD spake, saying, I will be sanctified in them that come nigh me, and before all the people I will be glorified. And Aaron held his peace.

Leviticus 10:2-3

Fifteen Restrictions of Anointed People

1. **An anointed person must not have much to do with the dead.**

And the LORD said unto Moses, Speak unto the priests the sons of Aaron, and say unto them, There shall none be defiled for the dead among his people:

Leviticus 21:1

Dead things contaminate the anointing. Death is one of the greatest enemies of God and will be dealt with at the end. When that happens we will sing, "O death, where is thy sting? O grave, where is thy victory?" (1 Corinthians 15:55).

Jesus said, "Let the dead bury their dead." An anointed person has more to do with life than death. When you are truly anointed, you will not spend too much time dabbling with death, funerals, wake-keepings, memorial services and all the rituals that go with death.

2. **An anointed person must have a covering.**

They shall not make baldness upon their head...

Leviticus 21:5

Baldness, (a lack of hair) speaks of the lack of a covering. Paul stated that the hair was a symbol of the covering of a person.

But if a woman have long hair, it is a glory to her: for her hair is given her for a covering.

1 Corinthians 11:15

All ministers should have a covering over their heads. There should be somebody you look up to and from whom you derive spiritual direction and inspiration.

The existence of such people over you in the ministry, from whom you derive guidance and inspiration, provides an important covering for your life.

3. **An anointed person is restricted in his physical appearance.**

    ...neither shall they shave off the corner of their beard, nor make any cuttings in their flesh.

    Leviticus 21:5

Unusual trimmings of the beard and marks on the flesh would make a priest look bizarre and even frightening. When you are anointed, how you dress and appear will be guided by the Holy Spirit.

The most anointed people like Elijah and John the Baptist had a peculiar appearance which seems to have been dictated by the anointing. That is why both John the Baptist and Elijah had the same appearance; because they carried the same anointing. In fact, they were recognized by their unusual appearance.

And he said unto them, What manner of man was he which came up to meet you, and told you these words? And they answered him, He was an hairy man, and girt with a girdle of leather about his loins. And he said, It is Elijah the Tishbite.

2 Kings 1:7,8

4. **Anointed men are restricted in the type of woman they marry.**

    They shall not take a wife that is a whore, or profane; neither shall they take a woman put away from her husband: for he is holy unto his God. And he shall take a wife in her VIRGINITY. A WIDOW, or a DIVORCED WOMAN, or PROFANE, or AN HARLOT, these shall he not take: but he shall take a virgin of his own people to wife.

    Leviticus 21:7,13-14

Because of the anointing on your life you cannot just marry anyone you want. Many ministries are aborted because this principle is overlooked. Perhaps this should be one of the easiest principles to relate with because marriage is well known to make or break a ministry.

5. **An anointed person must be as perfect as possible.**

    Speak unto Aaron, saying, Whosoever he be of thy seed in their generations that hath ANY BLEMISH, let him not approach to offer the bread of his God.

    Leviticus 21:17

Any kind of physical blemish disqualified a person from being a priest. Paul gives a parallel instruction when he says to Timothy that a bishop must be blameless.

6. **An anointed person must not be spiritually blind.**

    For whatsoever man he be that hath a blemish, he shall not approach: A BLIND MAN...or that hath a BLEMISH IN HIS EYE...

    Leviticus 21:18,20

A priest must not be spiritually blind. The absence of visions and dreams in a person's life often speaks of the absence of the Holy Spirit. An anointed person will have a minimal amount of supernatural sight even if he is not a prophet.

7. **An anointed person must not be spiritually immobile.**

For whatsoever man he be that hath a blemish, he shall not approach...OR A LAME...

Leviticus 21:18

Following God often involves moving along with the Spirit. The Spirit is always moving. If you cannot or do not move with the Holy Spirit, you become useless to Him because you fall out of step. Sluggishness in spiritual things will leave you far behind God's agenda.

8. **An anointed person must be spiritually sensitive.**

For whatsoever man he be that hath a blemish, he shall not approach...or he that hath A FLAT NOSE...

Leviticus 21:18

A flat nose speaks of someone whose ability to smell or sense things is affected. Sensitivity to the Holy Spirit is vital for an anointed person. A spiritually flat nose will not help the anointing.

9. **An anointed person must not have excesses.**

For whatsoever man he be that hath a blemish, he shall not approach...or ANY THING SUPERFLUOUS,

Leviticus 21:18

A man of God cannot have what is superfluous. An anointed man is restricted because he is anointed. He is not allowed to have certain excesses, which normal people may engage in. When you are anointed you cannot eat as much as you want to. You cannot have a lifestyle with the excesses that many non-anointed people indulge in. You may be restricted in what you eat, drink, buy, wear, drive, live in and do. What a small price to pay to be an anointed person.

10. **An anointed person must be able to go anywhere and do anything the Lord wants.**

For whatsoever man he be that hath a blemish, he shall not approach...Or a man that is BROKENFOOTED, or BROKENHANDED,

Leviticus 21:18,19

Broken feet and broken hands put limits on where you can go and what you can do.

If you are anointed, you cannot restrict God in what He will use you for. There are people who want to be anointed but also want to dictate to God what they will do in the kingdom. A broken foot and a broken hand limit what you do and where you can go.

As soon as the anointing comes on your life, you are His servant and you will go where He says you will go and do what He says you must do. You cannot say you are above the work of a secretary if that is what He wants you to do.

11. **An anointed person must not fail to develop and continue growing.**

     For whatsoever man he be that hath a blemish, he shall not approach...Or CROOKBACKT, or A DWARF...

Leviticus 21:18,20

A hunchback or a dwarf speak of someone whose growth has stalled. Spiritual dwarfs are people who have stopped growing. Being anointed requires even more spiritual growth and development. You cannot stop developing yourself and growing in the Spirit because you realize that God has anointed you.

I have to spend even more time developing myself because I am anointed.

12. **An anointed person must not have unhealed wounds.**

     For whatsoever man he be that hath a blemish, he shall not approach...or be SCURVY, or SCABBED, or hath his stones broken;

Leviticus 21:18,20

People with spiritual scurvy have unhealed wounds. Scurvy is the famous illness caused by the lack of vitamin C. In this illness, the main problem is the inability of the body to heal. Patients are sometimes given vitamin C to promote wound healing. A scab is also a kind of wound.

Every minister must be healed of the numerous wounds in his life and ministry. You must not minister out of your wounds and hurts. When you minister from your wounds, unforgiveness and bitterness take root in your soul.

13. Anointed people must stay in their calling.

And Nadab and Abihu, the sons of Aaron, took either of them his censer, and put fire therein, and put incense thereon, and OFFERED STRANGE FIRE before the LORD, which he commanded them not. And there went out fire from the LORD, and devoured them, and they died before the LORD.

Leviticus 10:1-2

An anointed person cannot offer strange fire which the Lord has not asked him for. Strange fire is something that God has not asked you to offer. You cannot switch from being a pastor to being a prophet if God does not require that from you. You cannot change your ministry and do anything within the church just because it is a good thing. Nadab and Abihu paid with their lives for doing things in the church that God had not asked them to do.

14. Anointed people cannot go back to the world. Their lives belong to God.

And YE SHALL NOT GO OUT FROM THE DOOR OF THE TABERNACLE of the congregation, lest ye die: for the anointing oil of the LORD is upon you. And they did according to the word of Moses.

Leviticus 10:7

Anointed people are restricted to the tabernacle. This is why many who are called by God sense that they will die if they leave the ministry. They know their lives are restricted to God's house and His service. That is why Paul said, "Woe is me if I preach not the gospel" (1Corinthians 9:16). He sensed death outside the tabernacle.

He knew he was doomed if he ventured outside the ministry God had given him.

15. Anointed people must only be influenced by the Holy Spirit.

DO NOT DRINK WINE NOR STRONG DRINK, thou, nor thy sons with thee, when ye go into the tabernacle of the congregation, lest ye die...

Leviticus 10:9

Spiritual people cannot afford to subject themselves to wrong influences. Wine and strong drink are influences that guide the behaviour of a person. An anointed person must be under the influence of the Holy Spirit.

It is the Holy Spirit who guides the ministry. Every ministry that is guided by secular and human wisdom is in great danger. The Holy Spirit has been given to help us walk through the darkness of our generation.

Chapter 14

The Kingly Anointing

Then Samuel took a vial of oil, and poured it upon his head, and kissed him, and said, Is it not because the LORD hath anointed thee to be captain over his inheritance?

1 Samuel 10:1

The kingly anointing is the anointing that ushered people into the office of a king. It is the anointing that turned an ordinary person into a king of Israel. The two greatest examples of the kingly anointing are seen in David and Saul.

The anointing that was poured upon David is discussed extensively in the chapter on the Lord's anointed. You will notice how King Saul rose to a place of authority through the anointing.

The Lord sent Samuel to anoint Saul, an ordinary person and the effect of this kingly anointing upon Saul is the subject for discussion in this chapter. You will see how Saul was completely transformed into a different person and was exalted because of the anointing.

You may ask, "What does this kingly anointing have to do with us?" Well, God has called us to be kings and priests unto Him.

And from Jesus Christ, who is the faithful witness, and the first begotten of the dead, and the prince of the kings of the earth. Unto him that loved us, and washed us from our sins in his own blood, And hath MADE US KINGS AND PRIESTS unto God and his Father...

Revelation 1:5-6

It is only by the anointing that you will fulfil this calling to authority and true kingship.

Fifteen Powerful Effects of the Kingly Anointing

1. **After you are anointed, you will recover things you have lost.**

   When thou art departed from me today, then thou shalt find two men by Rachel's sepulchre in the border of Benjamin at Zelzah; and they will say unto thee, The asses which thou wentest to seek are found: and, lo, thy father hath left the care of the asses, and sorroweth for you, saying, What shall I do for my son?

   1 Samuel 10:2

2. **The kingly anointing will make you go forward and make progress in life.**

   Then shalt thou go on forward from thence, and thou shalt come to the plain of Tabor, and there shall meet thee three men going up to God to Bethel, one carrying three kids, and another carrying three loaves of bread, and another carrying a bottle of wine.

   1 Samuel 10:3

3. **The kingly anointing will make men salute you.**

   You will no longer be ignored and disregarded. Those who despised you will be forced to reckon with you.

   And they will salute thee...

   1 Samuel 10:4

4. **The kingly anointing will cause men to give to you.**

   It is because of the anointing that men will come to you with gifts and offerings.

   ...and give thee two loaves of bread; which thou shalt receive of their hands.

   1 Samuel 10:4

5. You will go to God's presence.

You will find yourself spending more time in the house of God because of the anointing on your life.

After that thou shalt come to the hill of God...

1 Samuel 10:5

6. The anointing will set you up to meet certain people.

You are now destined to meet certain spiritual men who will sharpen your ministry. When their mantle combines with yours, your spiritual authority will be multiplied.

...thou shalt meet a company of prophets coming down from the high place with a psaltery, and a tabret, and a pipe, and a harp, before them; and they shall prophesy:

1 Samuel 10:5

7. The kingly anointing will make you prophesy.

To prophesy is to speak under the guidance or the inspiration of the Holy Spirit. You will definitely speak under inspiration of the Holy Spirit because of the anointing.

And the Spirit of the Lord will come upon thee, and thou shalt prophesy with them...

1 Samuel 10:6

8. You will be transformed into another man.

People who knew you before you were anointed will be unable to relate with you in your transformed status.

...and shalt be turned into another man.

1 Samuel 10:6

9. You will do as occasion serve thee.

...that thou do as occasion serve thee...

1 Samuel 10:7

You will take decisions naturally and flow with God as you go along. Your decisions will be inspired by the Spirit of God from the day that you receive the kingly anointing. That is why you can do "as occasion serve thee".

10. Your heart will be changed.

...God gave him another heart...

1 Samuel 10:9

Without a change of heart, you cannot receive the anointing nor use it. God had to give Saul another heart with which he could carry the anointing.

11. Your calling will be questioned.

You cannot enter the ministry without being challenged, questioned and resisted. Such things are to be expected at the beginning of your ministry.

> **And it came to pass, when all that knew him beforetime saw that, behold, he prophesied among the prophets, then the people said one to another, What is this that is come unto the son of Kish? Is Saul also among the prophets?**
>
> **And one of the same place answered and said, But who is their father? Therefore it became a proverb, Is Saul also among the prophets?**

1 Samuel 10:11-12

12. The kingly anointing will cause some people to support you.

> **And Samuel said to all the people, See ye him whom the Lord hath chosen, that there is none like him among all the people? And all the people shouted, and said, God save the king.**

1 Samuel 10:24

13. Some people's hearts will be touched to follow you.

And Saul also went home to Gibeah; and there went with him a band of men, whose hearts God had touched.

1 Samuel 10:26

14. The kingly anointing will stir up opposition.

But the children of Belial said, How shall this man save us?

1 Samuel 10:27

The sons of Satan are equally inspired to oppose every new thing that God does. Without opposition, you should even question your calling. The presence of opposition is a sign of God's calling and anointing.

15. The kingly anointing will stir up despisement.

...And they despised him, and brought him no presents. But he held his peace.

1 Samuel 10:27

Some people will not honour you with gifts and offerings in spite of what God does with your life. Scoffers and mockers are a normal feature on the road to the anointing. Take heart and press on. God has also touched the hearts of several people who will support you.

Chapter 15

The Anointing of Prophet Isaiah

Isaiah prophesied of the coming of the Spirit of the Lord upon him. In one of the most beautiful chapters of the Bible, he outlines the powerful effects that the coming of the Sprit of God would have. He declares that the Spirit of the Lord (the anointing) would be upon him and would make him do certain things, and would also make certain things happen.

When the anointing comes on you, it will also make you do certain things. Let us look at fifteen powerful effects of Isaiah's anointing.

1. **"The Spirit of the Lord GOD is upon me; because the LORD hath anointed me to preach good tidings unto the meek..." (Isaiah 61:1).**

The anointing will enable you to preach to the poor. It is the anointing that will release the finances that enable you to preach to people who cannot pay for the Gospel.

2. **"...he hath sent me to bind up the brokenhearted..." (Isaiah 61:1).**

The anointing on your life will cause your preaching and ministry to heal broken-hearted and disappointed people. Even though you may have no practical solutions for their problems, the anointing will heal their broken and disappointed hearts. This is why poor multitudes flock to churches that have an anointed pastor. He may not have husbands to give the lonely widows, but the anointing heals their broken hearts.

3. **"...to proclaim liberty to the captives, and the opening of the prison to them that are bound" (Isaiah 61:1).**

The anointing on your life will cause people that are bound to be set free. Many people are bound through the presence of evil spirits. Logical teaching and systematic lectures cannot open prison doors. It is by the anointing that freedom will come to those you minister to.

4. "...to comfort all that mourn" (Isaiah 61:2).

Comforting people that are mourning is part of the ministry of the Spirit. When you are anointed, people will be encouraged by just seeing you!

They will be encouraged when they hear you! They will be encouraged when you lay hands on them!

The fact that someone is encouraged does not mean he is healed. Sometimes there are legal reasons why people cannot be healed in this life and this comforting ministry is therefore a powerful alternative for them.

This comforting effect is very different from the healing anointing! The power of God that comforts without actually healing the problem is equally powerful. May people be encouraged and comforted when you speak or minister to them.

5. "...to give unto them beauty for ashes..." (Isaiah 61:3).

The anointing will restore your beauty and attractiveness. When that anointing is upon a pastor, many people are attracted to his church without knowing why. When the anointing is upon an evangelist many people are attracted to his crusades without knowing why.

Anointed people are beautiful. Non-anointed people have to spend a lot of money to make themselves look good. The anointing will make you fresh, beautiful, and attractive. Unfortunately, people do not realize when they are being attracted to an anointed person.

Through accusations, they shy away from anointed people, thinking they are desirous of something that is not theirs. They do not realize that the anointing has made the person attractive and they are in fact responding to the anointing on the person.

6. **"...the oil of joy for mourning, the garment of praise for the spirit of heaviness..." (Isaiah 61:3).**

The anointing will make you joyful. This is a reality. The spirit of heaviness is the spirit of depression. The feelings of depression (worthlessness, hopelessness and guilt) are not inspired by the Holy Spirit. They are often demonic affectations. When the anointing is on your life, you will have joy, praise and thankfulness in your heart.

7. **"...that they might be called trees of righteousness, the planting of the LORD, that he might be glorified" (Isaiah 61:3).**

The anointing will cause you to be a righteous person. Righteousness and holiness are not things that are easy to practise. Most human beings are unable to gain control over their passions and human weaknesses. There are many ministers who boast of their moral uprightness. They secretly think it is their principles and respectable lifestyle that guarantee righteousness. It takes a depth of spiritual insight to realize that it is actually the anointing that makes you a tree of righteousness.

8. **"And they shall build the old wastes, they shall raise up the former desolations, and they shall repair the waste cities, the desolations of many generations" (Isaiah 61:4).**

The anointing will enable you to build and to restore things. You will have the ability to raise up foundations and establish the work of God. You will have the ability to lay brick upon brick.

Because of the anointing, you will take lives that are shattered and hopeless and make something out of them. Years ago, I appointed someone as a pastor.

When another minister heard about this fellow becoming a pastor, he was amazed and said, "Dag is doing wonders." He could not believe that such a person could be lifted by the anointing into the ministry.

9. **"And strangers shall stand and feed your flocks, and the sons of the alien shall be your plowmen and your vinedressers" (Isaiah 61:5).**

The anointing will cause you to reach beyond your own country, your own tribe and nation. Some people are international ministers and fathers. Others are simply ministers for their country. Others are ministers for certain tribes and languages.

It takes the anointing to reach beyond your borders and affect foreigners. In the natural, people do not respond much to people who do not have their colour or accent. It takes the anointing to break these barriers.

10. **"But ye shall be named the Priests of the LORD: men shall call you the Ministers of our God..." (Isaiah 61:6).**

Because of the anointing you will be a priest. What an honour and privilege to be called a priest of the Lord. What on earth could make someone like you or me have such an honourable and holy vocation? Only the anointing could do such a thing!

11. **"...ye shall eat the riches of the Gentiles, and in their glory shall ye boast yourselves" (Isaiah 61:6).**

The anointing attracts wealth (and its attendant persecution). This is why many ministers of God are very wealthy. The riches and glory of the Gentiles speak of amazing wealth that comes to the anointed. No one should seek these riches nor the glory thereof. What we must seek is God and the anointing of the Holy Spirit. However, it is simply a reality that the anointing causes wealth to come into the hands of the anointed.

12. **"For your shame ye shall have double; and for confusion they shall rejoice in their portion: therefore in their land they shall possess the double: everlasting joy shall be unto them" (Isaiah 61:7).**

The anointing removes the shame of your past. Many shameful men and women with an appalling and reprehensible past now stand behind pulpits on Sunday mornings. The anointing has removed the shocking and scandalous past. The spirit of shame and disgrace is bound and they have become men and women of honour and even admiration.

The anointing removes confusion. Confusion is a spirit that harasses good people who try to serve the Lord. Confusion is ministered through powerful accusations that sound true. As the anointing comes upon you, shame and confusion depart.

13. **"And their seed shall be known among the Gentiles, and their offspring among the people: all that see them shall acknowledge them, that they are the seed which the LORD hath blessed" (Isaiah 61:9).**

The anointing will cause your children and descendants to be blessed. Throughout the Bible, it is clear that God's power affects the descendants of the anointed.

Make a demand on the anointing and expect your children to be helped because of the anointing on your life.

14. **"I will greatly rejoice in the LORD, my soul shall be joyful in my God; for he hath clothed me with the garments of salvation, he hath covered me with the robe of righteousness, as a bridegroom decketh himself with ornaments, and as a bride adorneth herself with her jewels" (Isaiah 61:10).**

The anointing will clothe you with garments of salvation. An anointed person is greatly concerned about salvation. He understands salvation. He marvels at salvation. He speaks about salvation. He preaches salvation and he ministers for people to be saved.

When the anointing is departed, the garment of salvation is removed and salvation is no longer a priority in the ministry.

In the book of Acts, the sign of the presence of the Holy Spirit was that the disciples would be empowered to be witnesses of Christ and His salvation.

Truly, the absence of the Holy Spirit changes the church dramatically and makes it a place where salvation does not occur.

15. **"For as the earth bringeth forth her bud, and as the garden causeth the things that are sown in it to spring forth; so the Lord GOD will cause righteousness and praise to spring forth before all the nations" (Isaiah 61:11).**

The anointing will cause righteousness to increase in the world. The anointing will cause praise to be offered to the Lord in many nations.

It is only the anointing of the Holy Spirit that can bring about the formation of churches and congregations who lift up the name of the Lord regularly.

Chapter 16

What it Means to Be the Lord's Anointed

To be the Lord's anointed is one of the greatest blessings a human being could ever have.

King David was anointed as a youth. He had absolutely nothing that would qualify him for the great position he came to occupy. The new thing in his life was the anointing by Samuel. Going forward, he therefore attributed everything to the anointing he had received. He virtually changed his name and called himself "the Lord's anointed". In his psalms and songs he always refers to himself as "the Lord's anointed".

The Benefits of Being the Lord's Anointed

1. **"Why do the heathen rage, and the people imagine a vain thing?...against the LORD, and against his anointed..." (Psalms 2:1-2).**

One day, I heard somebody praying an interesting prayer. He said, "I cancel all decisions that are taken against me."

I realized then that people meet and take decisions against the Lord's anointed. Their wicked schemes and ideas against your life will amount to nothing because of the anointing. That is why David asked why people even imagine such futile things.

What a blessing it is to be anointed! All meetings that are held to plan and to take decisions against your life will amount to nothing in Jesus' name.

2. **"...and sheweth mercy to his anointed..." (Psalms 18:50).**

A man of God is still a man. No matter how God uses you, you will need His mercy. Because of the precious ointment on your life, you can expect the mercy of God when you fall into sin.

David was a human being and he fell into sin many times. But he knew that the Lord would show mercy to his anointed. What a blessing it is to be anointed.

3. "Now know I that the Lord saveth his anointed..." (Psalm 20:6).

King David fought many battles. Perhaps he had almost lost his life on many occasions and he knew how easy it was to get killed. He himself said, that there is just a step between life and death.

And David sware moreover, and said, Thy father certainly knoweth that I have found grace in thine eyes; and he saith, Let not Jonathan know this, lest he be grieved: but truly as the LORD liveth, and as thy soul liveth, there is but a step between me and death.

1 Samuel 20:3

David believed that it was the anointing that had kept him from dying. Because you are the Lord's anointed, He will save you from sin and temptation. He will give you the upper hand in the day of your crisis. He will save you from falling into the hands of those that hate you. The anointed psalmist said, "Now know I that the Lord saveth His anointed."

4. "Thou lovest righteousness, and hatest wickedness: Therefore God, thy God, hath anointed thee with the oil of gladness above thy fellows" (Psalms 45:7).

The Lord's anointed is a happy person. The anointing makes you glad. All your sadness will be taken away because of the anointing. What a joy it is to serve the Lord. The futility and emptiness of this life is taken away by the anointing. Any reason for depression is taken away. The anointing is the oil of gladness.

5. "But my horn shalt thou exalt like the horn of an unicorn: I shall be anointed with fresh oil" (Psalms 92:10).

Your horn being exalted speaks of God establishing you as a man of authority. The anointing is what gives you spiritual authority.

Men will obey you even unto death because of the authority God has given you. Without the anointing, your words will carry no power and no one will listen to you. With the anointing even little instructions will be obeyed.

6. "Mine eye also shall see my desire on mine enemies..." (Psalms 92:11).

Your wishes for your enemies will come to pass because of the anointing. Those that torment you will be destroyed. You will see the end of those that hate you. You will hear of their funerals and burial services but you will live long and do the works of God.

7. "The righteous shall flourish like the palm tree: he shall grow like a cedar in Lebanon" (Psalms 92:12).

The anointing will make you increase and prosper in whatever you do. It is indeed the grace of God that causes a man to flourish when others just deteriorate. The flourishing of a palm tree is unusual because a palm tree can survive almost anywhere.

When the anointing is on you, your ministry will flourish everywhere. You may be in a small town but God will cause you to thrive. You may be in a poor city but because of the anointing, you will flourish and prosper.

You may have been sent to a place of no earthly significance but because of the palm tree anointing you will still succeed and become a fruitful ministry.

Those that be planted in the house of the LORD shall flourish in the courts of our God.

Psalms 92:13

Remember that you will flourish in the courts of God. If you move out of your calling, do not expect to flourish. When you leave the ministry, do not expect to flourish. God's promise is for you to flourish within His courts.

8. "They shall still bring forth fruit in old age; they shall be fat and flourishing" (Psalms 92:14).

When you are the Lord's anointed, you will bring forth fruit even in your old age. God has designed all His creation to have a short season of fruitfulness. But even when the youthful season of fruitfulness is gone, the anointing will cause you to thrive.

Many ministers experience great success at the beginning of ministry but end in tragedy, misery and smallness. When you are the Lord's anointed, your ministry will extend beyond a few youthful years of fruitfulness.

9. "...Touch not mine anointed, and do my prophets no harm" (Psalms 105:15).

The anointing creates an invisible covering and shield of protection. Many people hate the Lord's anointed and criticize him. When you are anointed, people will discuss you and invent stories about you! You will hear all kinds of things about yourself.

Perhaps it is a natural temptation to criticize the Lord's anointed, but God gives a very stern warning to all and sundry: "Do not touch my anointed!"

Many there are who have discovered how dangerous it is to touch the Lord's anointed.

How sad it is that aspiring ministers engage in much criticism about people whom the Lord has anointed. Perhaps this is the one seed which undermines their entire life and ministry – the fact that they have touched the Lord's anointed.

10. "...I have ordained a lamp for mine anointed" (Psalms 132:17).

God has provided a special lamp which directs His anointed. This lamp will guide the anointed person in the darkness of his life.

Expect illumination! Expect visions! Expect dreams! Expect special insight to the Word of God because of the anointing that is on your life. Often I feel the very presence of the Spirit when I read the Bible.

May you become an anointed servant of the Lord and may somebody call you "the Lord's anointed".

Chapter 17

Steps to Losing the Anointing

Saul is one of the beautiful Bible examples of someone who received the anointing. Unfortunately, he is also a sad example of someone who lost the anointing. Not only did he lose the anointing but evil spirits invaded his soul. A study of his life will reveal how he lost the precious gift and position he had.

Then came the word of the LORD unto Samuel, saying,

It repenteth me that I have set up Saul to be king: for he is turned back from following me, and hath not performed my commandments. And it grieved Samuel; and he cried unto the LORD all night.

And when Samuel rose early to meet Saul in the morning, it was told Samuel, saying, Saul came to Carmel, and, behold, he set him up a place, and is gone about, and passed on, and gone down to Gilgal. And Samuel came to Saul: and Saul said unto him, Blessed be thou of the LORD: I have performed the commandment of the LORD.

And Samuel said, What meaneth then this bleating of the sheep in mine ears, and the lowing of the oxen which I hear?

And Saul said, They have brought them from the Amalekites: for the people spared the best of the sheep and of the oxen, to sacrifice unto the LORD thy God; and the rest we have utterly destroyed.

Then Samuel said unto Saul, Stay, and I will tell thee what the LORD hath said to me this night. And he said unto him, Say on.

And Samuel said, When thou wast little in thine own sight, wast thou not made the head of the tribes of Israel, and the LORD anointed thee king over Israel?

And the LORD sent thee on a journey, and said, Go and utterly destroy the sinners the Amalekites, and fight against them until they be consumed. Wherefore then didst thou not obey the voice of the LORD, but didst fly upon the spoil, and didst evil in the sight of the LORD?

And Saul said unto Samuel, Yea, I have obeyed the voice of the LORD, and have gone the way which the LORD sent me, and have brought Agag the king of Amalek, and have utterly destroyed the Amalekites. But the people took of the spoil, sheep and oxen, the chief of the things which should have been utterly destroyed, to sacrifice unto the LORD thy God in Gilgal.

And Samuel said, Hath the LORD as great delight in burnt offerings and sacrifices, as in obeying the voice of the LORD? Behold, to obey is better than sacrifice, and to hearken than the fat of rams.

For rebellion is as the sin of witchcraft, and stubbornness is as iniquity and idolatry. Because thou hast rejected the word of the LORD, he hath also rejected thee from being king. And Saul said unto Samuel, I have sinned: for I have transgressed the commandment of the LORD, and thy words: because I feared the people, and obeyed their voice.

Now therefore, I pray thee, pardon my sin, and turn again with me, that I may worship the LORD.

And Samuel said unto Saul, I will not return with thee: for thou hast rejected the word of the LORD, and the LORD hath rejected thee from being king over Israel.

And as Samuel turned about to go away, he laid hold upon the skirt of his mantle, and it rent.

And Samuel said unto him, The LORD hath rent the kingdom of Israel from thee this day, and hath given it to a neighbour of thine, that is better than thou. And also the Strength of Israel will not lie nor repent: for he is not a man, that he should repent.

1 Samuel 15:10-29

Steps to Prevent You from Losing the Anointing

Step 1: Don't disobey the specific commands of the Lord for your ministry.

To disobey God is to reject His commandments. If you sow a seed of rejection you will be rejected yourself. Saul had a specific charge to eliminate the Amalekites. His failure to do this specific duty led to him losing the anointing.

> **Then came the word of the LORD unto Samuel, saying, It repenteth me that I have set up Saul to be king: for he is turned back from following me, and hath not performed my commandments. And it grieved Samuel; and he cried unto the LORD all night.**
>
> **1 Samuel 15:10-11**

Step 2: Don't become big in your own eyes.

Saul was anointed when he was small in his own eyes. It is important to continue to see yourself as little, unimportant and insignificant in order to maintain the anointing in your life.

> **And Samuel said, When thou wast little in thine own sight, wast thou not made the head of the tribes of Israel, and the LORD anointed thee king over Israel?**
>
> **1 Samuel 15:17**

Saul was made the head when he saw himself as little. The surest way to lose your leadership in ministry is to stop seeing yourself as a little nobody.

Step 3: Don't become interested in the financial and earthly benefits of ministry.

Saul jumped onto the benefits of his war with the Amalekites and grabbed what he could. This angered the Lord because he had developed an interest in other things.

> **And the Lord sent thee on a journey, and said, Go and utterly destroy the sinners the Amalekites, and fight**

against them until they be consumed. Wherefore then didst thou not obey the voice of the LORD, but didst fly upon the spoil, and didst evil in the sight of the LORD?

1 Samuel 15:18-19

Step 4: Don't sacrifice instead of obeying God.

And Samuel said, Hath the LORD as great delight in burnt offerings and sacrifices, as in obeying the voice of the LORD? Behold, to obey is better than sacrifice, and to hearken than the fat of rams.

1 Samuel 15:22

Doing all sorts of difficult and sacrificial things for God rather than listening to the voice of the Spirit angers God and leads to the anointing being leaked out. It is common as the ministry develops to want to do certain things that you know to be sacrificial rather than listening to the direction of the Lord.

It will surprise you to know that some of the directives of the Lord will actually be easy and even pleasurable to do. Failure to do these "easy" things is a common reason for losing your place and the anointing.

Step 5: Avoid rebellion and witchcraft.

For rebellion is as the sin of witchcraft, and stubbornness is as iniquity and idolatry. Because thou hast rejected the word of the LORD, he hath also rejected thee from being king.

1 Samuel 15:23

Saul was rebuked for witchcraft and rebellion. Witchcraft is the use of other powers to control people. Unfortunately, some ministers can use other powers apart from the Holy Spirit to control people. They are pushed around by manipulative powers, and other controls such as curses and accusations.

Step 6: Don't be stubborn.

He, that being often reproved hardeneth his neck, shall suddenly be destroyed, and that without remedy.

Proverbs 29:1

Saul was also rebuked for stubbornness. Stubbornness has to do with an unyielding and resistant spirit. Someone who needs repeated counselling and prodding to do the right thing is stubborn. Such people have to be rebuked over and over and need countless and diverse methods of communication which yield very little.

Like Saul, they never agree that they have sinned. They never say "yes", they never say "no", they never give up, they never give in, they never bow, they never yield, and they never bend - because they are stubborn. May you not be difficult to reach and difficult to communicate with. It is a sure way to lose the anointing. Try to understand issues quickly.

Step 7: Avoid iniquity.

All kinds of sin can make you lose the anointing. Sin opens the door for demons to come in. Sin becomes the foothold and the legal access of the enemy to your life. Jesus told us that the devil had no access to His life.

Hereafter I will not talk much with you: for the prince of this world cometh, and hath nothing in me.

John 14:30

Step 8: Avoid idolatry.

Samuel's famous rebuke of Saul was also for idolatry. Any kind of idol or god that comes between you and Jehovah will cause you to lose God's favour and anointing.

The history of the kings of Israel testifies to how God removes His grace when people follow idols.

Step 9: Don't fear the people.

And Saul said unto Samuel, I have sinned: for I have transgressed the commandment of the LORD, and thy words: because I feared the people, and obeyed their voice.

1 Samuel 15:24

Being afraid of people rather than being afraid of the Lord is a common cause of losing the anointing. It is important to fear God and not people.

As Though He Was Never Anointed

At the end of Saul's life, he was like someone who had never been anointed. He died the death of someone who had never experienced the grace of God.

David lamented:

The beauty of Israel is slain upon thy high places: how are the mighty fallen!

Tell it not in Gath, publish it not in the streets of Askelon; lest the daughters of the Philistines rejoice, lest the daughters of the uncircumcised triumph.

Ye mountains of Gilboa, let there be no dew, neither let there be rain, upon you, nor fields of offerings: for there the shield of the mighty is vilely cast away, the shield of Saul, as though he had not been anointed with oil.

2 Samuel 1:19-21

107

Chapter 18

The Road to the Anointing

Elisha, the Best Example

Elisha is the best example of someone who chose the anointing.

Elisha is the best example of someone who asked for the anointing.

Elisha is the best example of someone who received the anointing.

Elisha is the best example of someone who used the anointing.

Elisha is the best example of someone who received his spiritual mentor as a father.

Elisha is the best example of someone who served until he received the anointing.

Elisha is the best example of someone who was more anointed than his father.

In three remarkable verses of Scripture, we see the amazing revelation of how Elisha moved from being an ordinary ploughman to becoming the famous and extraordinary prophet who succeeded Elijah.

> **So he departed thence, and found Elisha the son of Shaphat, who was plowing with twelve yoke of oxen before him, and he with the twelfth: and Elijah passed by him, and cast his mantle upon him.**
>
> **And he left the oxen, and ran after Elijah, and said, Let me, I pray thee, kiss my father and my mother, and then I will follow thee. And he said unto him, Go back again: for what have I done to thee?**
>
> **And he returned back from him, and took a yoke of oxen, and slew them, and boiled their flesh with the instruments of the oxen, and gave unto the people, and they did eat. Then he arose, and went after Elijah, and ministered unto him.**
>
> **1 Kings 19:19-21**

Let us join Elisha on his road to the anointing. You can receive the anointing of the Holy Spirit if you walk the road Elisha walked. Everyone who walks on a particular road ends up at the same place. Roads do not lead to different places for different people!

Seven Steps on the Road to the Anointing

1. Accept the call eagerly.

And he left the oxen, and ran after Elijah...

1 Kings 19:20

It is important for you to accept the call of God. God calls many but not everyone accepts the call. Spouting a thousand and one excuses, they give themselves to other pursuits. Many whom God has called choose to live uneventful lives as "normal", moral, good Christians. In the name of being conscientious parents and responsible citizens, they choose to ignore the call of God.

These people receive a pat on the back from society and friends. They are applauded by the world as the "type" of Christian they want to see.

However, Elisha eagerly ran after the call. God is looking for people who respond eagerly to the offer of ministry.

2. Be a fighting man.

...and him that escapeth from the sword of Jehu SHALL ELISHA SLAY.

1 Kings 19: 17

Elisha was a man who could fight with the sword. The Christian life is a battle and the ministry is even more of a battle. Much of the fight goes on in the mind and in the form of temptations, ideas, imaginations, and alternatives to the will of God.

There will be continual pressure to fulfil your natural desires and instincts in the wrong way. Satan will present you with a cocktail of fantastic thoughts, suggestions, deceptions, and delusions. Until your very last day, an array of people, events and circumstances will present themselves as a complicated network of tests and temptations. Devils presenting themselves as angels and angels whom you suspect to be devils, will add to the confusion and the clamour of the battle on this earth. If you are not prepared to fight, you cannot have the anointing. Paul fought throughout his life and ministry. When he was dying he said, "I have fought a good fight." You will fight for every drop of the anointing that you ever receive. You will fight for every position that you ever occupy.

3. Be a ploughing man.

So he departed thence, and found Elisha the son of Shaphat, WHO WAS PLOWING with twelve yoke of oxen before him, and he with the twelfth...

1 Kings 19:19

Elisha was ploughing when he was called. Ploughing the ground speaks of hard work. Elisha was a hard-working and diligent person before he was called. The ministry is full of hard work that lasts for many years. Rarely does a lazy person amount to anything in the ministry.

4. Understand what it means when the mantle is thrown on you.

...and Elijah passed by him, and cast his mantle upon him.

1 Kings 19:19

It is important for you to understand what is happening in your life. The call of God is mysterious and may be vague. Exactly what God is saying and what He intends to do is often hidden from you. It is important to understand the gentle indications that God sends to you.

Elisha could have asked Elijah, "Why did you throw your mantle on me? What are you trying to say? Do you think I need some extra clothes?"

However, Elisha did not say any of those things. He knew what it meant. He lost interest in his oxen! He did not want his ploughing business anymore! His eyes were lifted up to something higher.

Sometimes when a mantle falls on you, you just have a desire to serve God and to live for him. Sometimes when a mantle falls on you, your interest in secular things dies. Nothing attracts you and no amount of money can lure you. These changes in your life are signs that a mantle has fallen on you.

5. Kill your oxen.

And he returned back from him, and took a yoke of oxen, and slew them, and boiled their flesh with the instruments of the oxen, and gave unto the people, and they did eat...

1 Kings 19:21

Everybody has something valuable when he is called. It is important to sacrifice what you have and to follow the call of God to its logical conclusion. Every call has a price. Do not think that you are going to have the anointing without paying as high a price as all anointed people do.

6. Leave your family.

...Let me, I pray thee, kiss my father and my mother, and then I will follow thee...

1 Kings 19:20

The call often involves some kind of separation from your family. Your family always pays a price for you to live out the call of God.

Many people have a priority list in which they say, God first, family second and then ministry third. I wonder where they got that list from. I do not agree with that priority list.

That is in conflict with what Jesus said.

If any man come to me, and hate not his father, and mother, and wife, and children, and brethren, and sisters, yea, and his own life also, he cannot be my disciple.

And whosoever doth not bear his cross, and come after me, cannot be my disciple.

Luke 14:26-27

Husbands, wives, children, brothers and sisters all pay a price because God has called you.

Although the cost of ministry is high, the cost of disobedience is even higher and this is what people do not know.

7. Serve the anointed man.

...Then he arose, and went after Elijah, and ministered unto him.

1 Kings 19:21

How necessary it is to humbly serve in the house of the Lord. Elisha was known to the public as the one who poured water on the hands of Elijah (2 Kings 3:11). The apostles were known as the servants and disciples of Christ. Joshua was known as the servant of Moses. Before you receive the depth of the anointing, you must become a servant.

Chapter 19

The Battle for the Double Portion

Elisha chose the anointing. He recognized that the greatest thing he could inherit from Elijah was the anointing. Sadly, many people do not realize that the source of all blessings is the anointing of the Holy Spirit. Elisha cheekily asked for a double portion of that precious gift. And he got it!

> **And it came to pass, when they were gone over, that Elijah said unto Elisha, Ask what I shall do for thee, before I be taken away from thee. And Elisha said, I pray thee, LET A DOUBLE PORTION OF THY SPIRIT BE UPON ME.**
>
> **2 Kings 2:9**

Receiving the anointing was not easy for Elisha. Elijah told him that he had made a difficult request. Elisha had to battle for the anointing; he had to battle to stay with Elijah. The battles took place in four locations: Gilgal, Jericho, Bethel and Jordan. Each of these four places is symbolic of something important on the road to the anointing.

The mention of each city brings memories of important spiritual events that took place in the Bible.

Fighting for a Double Portion in Gilgal

At Gilgal, Elijah tried to get rid of Elisha. This was a test to see whether Elisha would persist in his quest for the anointing.

> **And it came to pass, when the LORD would take up Elijah into heaven by a whirlwind, that Elijah went with Elisha from GILGAL.**
>
> **And Elijah said unto Elisha, Tarry here, I pray thee; for the LORD hath sent me to BETHEL. And Elisha said**

unto him, As the LORD liveth, and as thy soul liveth, I will not leave thee. So they went down to Bethel.

2 Kings 2:1-2

The Symbolic Meaning of Gilgal

1. Gilgal - The place of circumcision.

This is where the Israelites were circumcised before they crossed the Jordan. It symbolizes the pain of sacrifice: cutting away of the flesh, the painful cutting away of the world; painfully cutting away things you love.

> **And the people came up out of Jordan on the tenth day of the first month, AND ENCAMPED IN GILGAL, in the east border of Jericho.**

> **And those twelve stones, which they took out of Jordan, did JOSHUA PITCH IN GILGAL.**

> **And he spake unto the children of Israel, saying, When your children shall ask their fathers in time to come, saying, What mean these stones?**

> **Then ye shall let your children know, saying, Israel came over this Jordan on dry land.**

> **For the LORD your God dried up the waters of Jordan from before you, until ye were passed over, as the LORD your God did to the Red sea, which he dried up from before us, until we were gone over:**

> **That all the people of the earth might know the hand of the LORD, that it is mighty: that ye might fear the LORD your God for ever.**

> **And it came to pass, when all the kings of the Amorites, which were on the side of Jordan westward, and all the kings of the Canaanites, which were by the sea, heard that the LORD had dried up the waters of Jordan from before the children of Israel, until we were passed over, that their heart melted, neither was there spirit in them any more, because of the children of Israel.**

AT THAT TIME THE LORD SAID UNTO JOSHUA, MAKE THEE SHARP KNIVES, AND CIRCUMCISE again the children of Israel the second time.

And Joshua made him sharp knives, and circumcised the children of Israel at the hill of the foreskins.

And this is the cause why Joshua did circumcise: All the people that came out of Egypt, that were males, even all the men of war, died in the wilderness by the way, after they came out of Egypt.

Now all the people that came out were circumcised: but all the people that were born in the wilderness by the way as they came forth out of Egypt, them they had not circumcised.

Joshua 4:19-5:5

2. Gilgal - The place where the manna ceased.

The supernatural provision of manna ceased in Gilgal. From then on, the Israelites would have to sow and reap for themselves. They were no longer going to stumble into things accidentally. When you get to Gilgal, you will be expected to deliberately do the right things that lead to the anointing. We often stumble into many kingdom blessings. However, there comes a time when God expects you to deliberately work to get what you need.

You may have stumbled into the right church and enjoyed the ministry of a good pastor. But a time may come when God will expect you to deliberately choose a man of God to serve and to follow.

And the children of Israel ENCAMPED IN GILGAL, and kept the passover on the fourteenth day of the month at even in the plains of Jericho.

And they did eat of the old corn of the land on the morrow after the passover, unleavened cakes, and parched corn in the selfsame day.

AND THE MANNA CEASED on the morrow after they had eaten of the old corn of the land; neither had

the children of Israel manna any more; but they did eat
of the fruit of the land of Canaan that year.

Joshua 5:10-12

Fighting for a Double Portion in Bethel

In Bethel, other prophets tried to discourage Elisha and dissuade
him from following Elijah. Elijah himself advised Elisha to give
up his quest for the anointing and to stay away. But Elisha was
too clever to fall for this suggestion.

**And the sons of the prophets that were at BETHEL
came forth to Elisha, and said unto him, Knowest thou
that the LORD will take away thy master from thy
head to day? And he said, Yea, I know it; hold ye your
peace.**

**And Elijah said unto him, Elisha, tarry here, I pray
thee; for the LORD hath sent me to JERICHO. And he
said, As the LORD liveth, and as thy soul liveth, I will
not leave thee. So they came to Jericho.**

2 Kings 2:3-4

The Symbolic Meaning of Bethel

1. **Bethel - The place which takes you further away from
your vision.**

If you look on the map, you will find that going to Bethel meant
going further away from Jordan. Just as going to Bethel meant a
diversion from a direct path to Jordan, you may have to follow the
Spirit into places that may seem like a diversion. Dear brother,
there are times God's direction may seem very strange but it is all
part of the road to the anointing.

**And JACOB went out from Beer-sheba, and went
toward Haran.**

**And he lighted upon a certain place, and tarried there
all night, because the sun was set; and he took of the**

116

stones of that place, and put them for his pillows, and lay down in that place to sleep.

AND HE DREAMED, and behold a ladder set up on the earth, and the top of it reached to heaven: and behold the angels of God ascending and descending on it.

And, behold, the LORD stood above it, and said, I am the LORD God of Abraham thy father, and the God of Isaac: the land whereon thou liest, to thee will I give it, and to thy seed;

And thy seed shall be as the dust of the earth, and thou shalt spread abroad to the west, and to the east, and to the north, and to the south: and in thee and in thy seed shall all the families of the earth be blessed. And, behold, I am with thee, and will keep thee in all places whither thou goest, and will bring thee again into this land; for I will not leave thee, until I have done that which I have spoken to thee of.

And Jacob awaked out of his sleep, and he said, Surely the LORD is in this place; and I knew it not.

And he was afraid, and said, How dreadful is this place! this is none other but the house of God, and this is the gate of heaven.

And Jacob rose up early in the morning, and took the stone that he had put for his pillows, and set it up for a pillar, and poured oil upon the top of it.

And HE CALLED THE NAME OF THAT PLACE BETHEL: but the name of that city was called Luz at the first.

Genesis 28:10-19

2.   Bethel - The place of dreams and visions.

This is the place where Jacob had dreams and visions of God. When you come to Bethel you will have visions and dreams and God will direct you in more supernatural ways.

3. Bethel - The place of encountering God personally.

Bethel is the place where Jacob encountered God himself. He did not depend on Abraham's experience. He got to know God himself when he got to Bethel. When you get to Bethel, you will not depend on what someone says about God. You will begin to know Him for yourself. It will not be about what you have read or what you have watched. It will be about what you have experienced.

4. Bethel - The place of committing your finances to God.

It was at Bethel that Jacob committed his tithes to the Lord. Surprisingly, many men of God have difficulty in doing the right thing when it comes to finances. When you have been to Bethel, tithing will not be a problem for you.

> **And Jacob rose up early in the morning, and took the stone that he had put for his pillows, and set it up for a pillar, and poured oil upon the top of it.**
>
> **And he called the name of that place Bethel: but the name of that city was called Luz at the first.**
>
> **AND JACOB VOWED A VOW, saying, If God will be with me, and will keep me in this way that I go, and will give me bread to eat, and raiment to put on,**
>
> **So that I come again to my father's house in peace; then shall the LORD be my God:**
>
> **And this stone, which I have set for a pillar, shall be God's house: and of all that thou shalt give me I WILL SURELY GIVE THE TENTH UNTO THEE.**
>
> **Genesis 28:18-22**

5. Bethel - The place of making covenants with God.

It was at Bethel that Jacob made a covenant with God. He promised to serve Him and worship Him. He promised his tithes to God.

There comes a time in the ministry when you enter a deeper relationship with God. A marriage relationship is a deeper and higher relationship because of the covenants involved. Your ministry enters a new dimension when there are covenants between you and God.

Fighting for a Double Portion in Jericho

Once again, junior prophets and other anointed people tried to discourage Elisha. Elijah told Elisha that it was all over and that they needed to separate.

Elisha refused to leave the old man even though he knew they had come to the end. What is the point in following an old man who has no future? But that may be the road to the anointing.

> **And the sons of the prophets that were at JERICHO came to Elisha, and said unto him, Knowest thou that the LORD will take away thy master from thy head to day? And he answered, Yea, I know it; hold ye your peace.**
> **And Elijah said unto him, Tarry, I pray thee, here; for the LORD hath sent me to JORDAN. And he said, As the LORD liveth, and as thy soul liveth, I will not leave thee. And they two went on.**
>
> **2 Kings 2:5,6**

The Symbolic Meaning of Jericho

1. Jericho - The place of war.

This is the place where Joshua fought his first battle.

2. Jericho - The place for getting rid of disloyalty.

This is the place where disloyal people must be eliminated. The elders of Israel promised to kill anyone who murmured against Joshua.

This is a good place to get to. With the removal of disloyal traitors and liars you have the peace you need to build.

Whosoever he be that doth rebel against thy commandment, and will not hearken unto thy words in all that thou commandest him, he shall be put to death: only be strong and of a good courage.

Joshua 1:18

3. Jericho - The place of authority.

It is in Jericho that Joshua cursed anyone who would attempt to rebuild Jericho. His words came to pass because he had become a man of authority in Jericho. When you get to the Jericho of your ministry, you will become a man of authority.

In his days did Hiel the Bethelite build Jericho: he laid the foundation thereof in Abiram his firstborn, and set up the gates thereof in his youngest son Segub, according to the word of the LORD, which he spake by Joshua the son of Nun.

1 Kings 16:34

Fighting for a Double Portion in Jordan

Finally, they got to Jordan, the place of the anointing. Elisha had to ignore the staring eyes of fifty unanointed prophets. Under the intense glare of these other ministers, Elisha persisted with his vision of getting a double portion - and he got it.

And fifty men of the sons of the prophets went, and stood to view afar off: and they two stood by Jordan.

2 Kings 2:7

The Symbolic Meaning of Jordan

1. Jordan - The place where your desires are met.

Elisha's dream of receiving the double portion was fulfilled at the Jordan. Your dreams and visions will come to pass at Jordan.

2. Jordan - The place of spiritual vision.

Elisha's eyes were opened at the Jordan and he saw spiritual chariots and spiritual horses. This was a condition for him to receive the anointing: "If you see me!!" When you get to Jordan, you will begin to have important visions and dreams that will lead you to the heights of ministry.

> **And fifty men of the sons of the prophets went, and stood to view afar off: and they two stood by Jordan.**
>
> **And he said, Thou hast asked a hard thing: nevertheless, IF THOU SEE ME when I am taken from thee, it shall be so unto thee; but if not, it shall not be so.**
>
> **2 Kings 2:7,10**

Having spiritual eyes and spiritual vision is key to receiving the anointing.

The eyes of Peter, James and John were touched at the mount of transfiguration.

Paul's eyes were touched on the road to Damascus and he saw a bright light.

Jesus' eyes were opened and he saw a dove and heard a voice at Jordan. Every time you have a vision, you are being drawn nearer to the spirit realm.

3. Jordan - The place of alertness.

Spiritual alertness is important to receiving the anointing. Elisha was awake and alert when the spiritual chariots and horses were passing by. That is why he received the anointing.

People who sleep during powerful services often miss the moment the mantle falls. They are fast asleep when the chariots and horses come by. Forgive!

4. Jordan - The place of becoming a son with your father.

It is at Jordan that Elisha called Elijah his father. When you get to the place where you see your spiritual mentor as a father, you are qualified to receive the anointing.

You may initially see him as a friend or even a boss. But when he becomes your father, you are ready to receive the blessings of a son or a daughter.

5. Jordan - The place of rending your clothes and putting on the garb of your father.

This is the place where you take off your own identity and put on the identity of the spiritual person you are following. You will begin to look like him and act like him. John the Baptist looked like Elijah because he carried his anointing.

6. Jordan - The place where you receive the anointing.

Jesus was baptized and filled with the Spirit in the Jordan.

The Jordan was parted three times by heavily anointed people. The first time, the Jordan was parted by Joshua as he walked across with the people of Israel. The second time, the Jordan parted was when Elijha and Elisha crossed it together. The third time the Jordan was parted was when Elisha crossed back with the double portion he had just received.

May you come to Jordan where you receive the double portion of the anointing!

Chapter 20

The Life of the Anointed

1.   An anointed life is dedicated to God.

Elijah faithfully delivered difficult messages to the king. A truly anointed person does not mind how unpopular he becomes.

> **And Elijah the Tishbite, who was of the inhabitants of Gilead, said unto Ahab, As the Lord God of Israel liveth, before whom I stand, there shall not be dew nor rain these years, but according to my word.**
>
> **1 Kings 17:1**

2.   An anointed life is a life of paradoxes and contradictions.

Elijah had the power to stop rain but still needed to run and hide from the Queen.

> **Get thee hence, and turn thee eastward, and hide thyself by the brook Cherith, that is before Jordan.**
>
> **1 Kings 17:3**

3.   An anointed life is a life of paradoxes and contradictions.

Elijah, the anointed person, had power to hold back rain and power to make the rain fall. Yet, Elijah had no power to keep the river from drying up.

> **And it came to pass after a while, that the brook dried up, because there had been no rain in the land.**
>
> **1 Kings 17:7**

4.   An anointed life is a life of paradoxes and contradictions.

Elijah had power to hold back rain but no power to prevent a widow's son who lived with him from dying.

And it came to pass after these things, that the son of the woman, the mistress of the house, fell sick; and his sickness was so sore, that there was no breath left in him.

1 Kings 17:17

5. An anointed person will live and prosper in God's way.

God will decide how you get money and He will also decide how you will use it. Usually, anointed people are blessed with finances, but in a humbling way. Elijah was fed by ravens and widows. That is how God had chosen to bless him.

And THE RAVENS BROUGHT HIM BREAD and flesh in the morning, and bread and flesh in the evening; and he drank of the brook.

1 Kings 17:6

6. God commands supporters to believe in His anointed men!

God commands various people to love anointed men! God commands various people to help anointed men!

And the word of the LORD came unto him, saying,

Arise, get thee to Zarephath, which belongeth to Zidon, and dwell there: behold, I HAVE COMMANDED A WIDOW WOMAN THERE TO SUSTAIN THEE.

And she went and did according to the saying of Elijah: and she, and he, and her house, did eat many days

1 Kings 17:8-9,15

7. Anointed men have to endure being the minority.

Then said Elijah unto the people, I, even I only, remain a prophet of the LORD; but Baal's prophets are four hundred and fifty men.

1 Kings 18:22

8. Anointed men must overcome the "Jezebels" of their ministry.

The highest kind of anointing often attracts the spirit of Jezebel. Jezebel may manifest in different ways.

Jezebel may be a woman who uses her body to entice and seduce you.

> **And when Jehu was come to Jezreel, Jezebel heard of it; and SHE PAINTED HER FACE, and tired her head, and looked out at a window.**
>
> **And as Jehu entered in at the gate, she said, Had Zimri peace, who slew his master?**
>
> **And he lifted up his face to the window, and said, Who is on my side? who? And there looked out to him two or three eunuchs.**
>
> **And he said, Throw her down. So they threw her down: and some of her blood was sprinkled on the wall, and on the horses: and he trode her under foot.**
>
> **2 Kings 9:30-33**

Jezebel may be a woman who tries to control your ministry by eliminating those she does not like.

> **For it was so, when JEZEBEL CUT OFF THE PROPHETS of the LORD, that Obadiah took an hundred prophets, and hid them by fifty in a cave, and fed them with bread and water.**
>
> **1 Kings 18:4**

Jezebel may be a wife who manipulates and controls her husband's life and decisions.

> **But Jezebel his wife came to him, and said unto him, Why is thy spirit so sad, that thou eatest no bread?**
>
> **And he said unto her, Because I spake unto Naboth the Jezreelite, and said unto him, Give me thy vineyard for money; or else, if it please thee, I will give thee another**

vineyard for it: and he answered, I will not give thee my vineyard.

And Jezebel his wife said unto him, Dost thou now govern the kingdom of Israel? arise, and eat bread, and let thine heart be merry: I WILL GIVE THEE THE VINEYARD of Naboth the Jezreelite.

So SHE WROTE LETTERS in Ahab's name, and sealed them with his seal, and sent the letters unto the elders and to the nobles that were in his city, dwelling with Naboth.

And SHE WROTE IN THE LETTERS, saying, Proclaim a fast, and set Naboth on high among the people:

And set two men, sons of Belial, before him, to bear witness against him, saying, Thou didst blaspheme God and the king. And then carry him out, and stone him, that he may die.

And THE MEN OF HIS CITY, even the elders and the nobles who were the inhabitants in his city, DID AS JEZEBEL HAD SENT unto them, and as it was written in the letters which she had sent unto them.

1 Kings 21:5-11

Jezebel may also be a man who controls your ministry and your decisions.

Jezebel may also be a husband who manipulates and restricts his wife.

Chapter 21

How Will I Know When
I Am Anointed?

People often ask, "How will I know when I am anointed?" I think there are several biblical pointers that can help answer that question.

Eight Ways by Which You Can Know that You Are Anointed

1. When you begin to do certain things that your mentor/ father does, it is a sign you carry his anointing.

Elisha did many of the same kind of miracles that Elijah did. He actually did twice as many miracles because he had a double portion of his anointing.

One day, I realized I was writing books that were similar in direction and content to those of someone I had been following for years. This, to me, was a sign that I was carrying a certain anointing.

2. When people make particular comments about your preaching.

Almost every preacher has people commending him after he ministers. That is not what I am talking about and that is certainly not a sign that you are anointed.

However, there are certain remarks and comments that are made about anointed preaching. I always notice when those kind of remarks are made about people I know. To me, it is a sign that the anointing has began to seep into their ministries. Notice how these unusual remarks were made about Jesus' preaching ministry.

And it came to pass, when Jesus had ended these sayings, the people were ASTONISHED AT HIS DOCTRINE:

Matthew 7:28

And when the sabbath day was come, he began to teach in the synagogue: and **MANY HEARING HIM WERE ASTONISHED**, saying, From whence hath this man these things? and what wisdom is this which is given unto him, that even such mighty works are wrought by his hands?

Mark 6:2

And the scribes and chief priests heard it, and sought how they might destroy him: for they feared him, because ALL THE PEOPLE WAS ASTONISHED AT HIS DOCTRINE.

Mark 11:18

And all that heard him were ASTONISHED AT HIS UNDERSTANDING AND ANSWERS

Luke 2:47

And they were ASTONISHED at his doctrine: for HIS WORD WAS WITH POWER.

Luke 4:32

3. Healing is a sign that you are anointed.

You can raise your voice when preaching to stir up the congregation. You can also crack many jokes to make people happy with your sermons. All sorts of human tricks can be used to enhance preaching. However, you cannot conjure up genuine miracles. People are either healed or they are not. Healing is definitely a sign of the presence of the anointing.

How God anointed Jesus of Nazareth with the Holy Ghost and with power: who went about doing good,

and healing all that were oppressed of the devil; for God was with him.

Acts 10:38

4. Ministering to poor people is a sign of the anointing.

One sign of an anointed person is that he ministers to poor people. Most people minister in easily accessible cities and to people who can pay for good preaching.

However, preaching to the poor for whom the Gospel is ordained is a different matter. Most of us are guided by financial restraints and the absence of danger. Ministers know how good it feels to receive a fat honorarium and they love to go back to appreciative and rich congregations over and over again.

It takes a really anointed person to be guided by the Holy Spirit to minister amongst the poor.

The Spirit of the Lord is upon me, because he hath anointed me to preach the gospel to the poor...

Luke 4:18

5. Evangelism is a sign of the anointing.

Jesus specifically said that the sign of the presence of the Holy Spirit (the anointing) would be power to witness and evangelize.

But ye shall receive power, after that the Holy Ghost is come upon you: and ye shall be witnesses unto me both in Jerusalem, and in all Judaea, and in Samaria, and unto the uttermost part of the earth.

Acts 1:8

The absence of evangelism in many churches and ministries is a sign of the lack of the Holy Spirit (the anointing). The money-loving spirit of the world has replaced the Holy Spirit in the church!

6. Missions to the ends of the world is a sign of the anointing (the Holy Spirit).

The uttermost parts of the earth will hear the Gospel when the Holy Spirit comes. You will notice how the Holy Spirit (the anointing) drives the church to the ends of the world with the Gospel. The failure of the church to move out of its comfort zone into the remote corners of this world is surely a sign of the absence of the anointing (the Holy Spirit).

7. Travelling to minister is a sign of the anointing.

The Bible says that Jesus went about doing good and healing people. He did not stay in one place. He travelled to where the souls were. He went to many towns and villages doing the work of God. He did all these because He was anointed to travel and to bring deliverance and salvation to many.

8. Various good works are a sign of the anointing.

There are many non-specific good works that emanate from the anointing. The Bible teaches how Jesus went about DOING GOOD and healing all that were oppressed of the devil (Acts 10:38).

The anointing is the Holy Spirit, who is God. You cannot limit Him to doing particular things. Many people do different things because the anointing is on their lives.

The anointing can make you like someone (Mark 1:18).

The anointing can make you desire certain things (Philippians 2:13; 1 Timothy 2:1).

The anointing can make you lose interest in earthly things (Colossians 3:1-2).

The anointing can make you a helper (Exodus 31:2-5).

The anointing can make you a builder (Exodus 31:2-5).

The anointing can make you have wisdom (Isaiah 11:1).

The anointing gives you various abilities for various things (Exodus 31:3).

Chapter 22

Fulfil Your Ministry

Then he which had received the one talent came and said, Lord, I knew thee that thou art an hard man, reaping where thou hast not sown, and gathering where thou hast not strawed:

And I WAS AFRAID, and went and HID THY TALENT in the earth: lo, there thou hast that is thine.

His lord answered and said unto him, Thou WICKED and SLOTHFUL servant, thou knewest that I reap where I sowed not, and gather where I have not strawed:

Thou oughtest therefore to have put my money to the exchangers, and then at my coming I should have received mine own with usury.

Take therefore the talent from him, and give it unto him which hath ten talents.

For unto every one that hath shall be given, and he shall have abundance: but from him that hath not shall be taken away even that which he hath.

And cast ye the UNPROFITABLE SERVANT into outer darkness: there shall be weeping and gnashing of teeth.

Matthew 25:24-30

Once you have received the anointing, it is important to fulfil your ministry. The anointing is not for picnics, games and other pleasures. It is for the serious work of winning this world to Christ. Unfortunately, some people who receive the anointing do not fulfil their ministry and do not use the gift that they are given.

Seven Reasons Why Some People Do Not Fulfil Their Ministry

1. Not wanting to lose anything

They do not want to suffer loss. Unfortunately, the ministry is all about losing your life so that you can gain eternal rewards.

2. Not wanting another person to benefit without charge

The man with one talent did not want his hard master to receive something for doing nothing. This attitude keeps many out of the ministry. The ministry is all about doing things for people who have not paid for it. It is all about ministering to the poor, who receive expensive blessings at no charge.

3. Fear

The man who did not use his talents said, "I was afraid and I hid myself." Fear is a demon which keeps people away from fulfilling their ministry.

4. Hiding talents

"I hid myself", were the words of the unworthy servant. Hiding talents and gifts is a reason why people do not fulfil their ministry. When gifts are hidden, no one sees them and no one encourages them.

5. Wickedness

It is wickedness to withhold something that can benefit others. Many people have no love for people who are suffering and it is this wickedness which prevents them from giving to the needy.

6. Laziness

Sheer laziness keeps many people away from fulfilling their ministry. Ministry involves hard work. Lazy people have no place in the vineyard. Jesus told us to pray for labourers and not for holidaymakers!

7. Unprofitable Servants

This servant was a person who was not useful for anything in the church. He was not helpful, he did not contribute to anything, and he did not help to build anything. He was totally useless to the church! Useless people are dangerous people. If you are not faithful with little things, how will you be faithful with the anointing?

Dear friend, it is important for you to fulfil your ministry. The anointing has been given to you for a purpose. Do not be an unprofitable servant. Let us use the anointing and win this world for Jesus!

To the making of many books there is no end. May the words in this book help you find that precious anointing!

Books by
Dag Heward-Mills

CPSIA information can be obtained
at www.ICGtesting.com
Printed in the USA
FSOW04n1624100117
29486FS

9 789988 596231